LUMINOUS MOMENTS

THE CONTEMPORARY SACRED

LYN McCREDDEN

ATF PRESS

2010

National Library of Australia Cataloguing-in-Publication entry

Author: McCredden, Lyn, 1953-

Title: Luminous moments : the contemporary sacred / by Lyn McCredden.

ISBN: 9781921511950 (pbk.)

Notes: Includes index.

Subjects: Religion and culture.
Religion in literature.
Religion and literature.
Australian literature--History and criticism.
Sacred books.
Sacred music.
Spirituality.

Dewey Number: 201.7

Cover design by Simeon Nasilowski
Book layout by Astrid Sengkey

An imprint of the ATF Ltd
PO Box 504
Hindmarsh, SA 5007
ABN 90 116 359 963
www.atfpress.com

Contents

Acknowledgments

Acknowledgement is given to the following publication houses and journals, for permission to republish the following essays:

Antipodes, the *American Journal of Australasian Literary and Cultural Studies*, for permission to publish McCredden, Lyn 'Sacred violence in the Chamberlain case', in *Antipodes*, 22/2 (2008): 117–122.

'The Impossible Infinite: Les Murray, Poetry, and the Sacred', in *Antipodes* 19/2 (2005): 166–171.

Coolabah online journal for permission to publish McCredden, Lyn 'Forms of Memory in Post-colonial Australia', in *Coolabah: Perspectives: Myth, History and Memory*, 3 (2009): 60–67, Departament de Filologia Anglesa i Alemanya, Australian Studies Centre, University of Barcelona, Barcelona, Spain.

Australian Literary Studies, for permission to reprint:
'Contemporary Poetry and the Sacred: Vincent Buckley and Samuel Wagan Watson', in *Australian Literary Studies*, 23/2 153–167, University of Queensland Press, St Lucia, Queensland.

'"Untranscended / Life Itself": The Poetry of Pam Brown', in *Australian Literary Studies*, 22/2 217–228, University of Queensland Press, St Lucia, Qld

The Journal of Postcolonial Writing and Ashgate Publishing for permission to publish the article McCredden Lyn, 'The Carnal Theologies of Nick Cave', in Welberry, Karen and Dalziell, Tanya (eds), *Cultural Seeds : Essays*

on the Work of Nick Cave (Surrey: Ashgate Publishing Limited, 2009), 167–185.

Rodopi Publishers
'Sacred Exchange: Peter Carey's Oscar and Lucinda', in Andreas Gaile (ed), *Fabulating Beauty: Perspectives on the Fiction of Peter Carey* (Amsterdam - New York, Netherlands: Rodolphi, 2005), 171–178.

To all those colleagues and friends and family who have lent an ear, and their thoughts, to new ways of understanding the sacred. Thank you.

To my publisher ATF Press and in particular to Hilary Regan, who has always been positive and encouraging, and to Astrid Sengkey for her work on cover design and layout, thank you.

Introduction: The Pervasiveness of the Sacred

And the people bowed and prayed
To the neon god they made.
And the sign flashed out its warning
in the words that it was forming.
And the sign said: The words of the Prophets
are written on the Subway Walls
And tenement halls
And whispered in the sounds of silence.
('The Sounds of Silence', Jenkins and Simons, 1965)

no one
 on the corner
                    here

silent,
      not spiritual,
  the city is empty

antispectacular
     & as
  deodorised
           as heaven

no sleeping boys
         no density
  no belching
  pissing bodies
no spitting
 in the street
(Pam Brown, 'Pique', *50–50*, 67–70, 1997)

The word *sacred* embraces the long history of human desires for (and against) ultimate meaning. It is a capacious enough word, I hope, to indicate the diverse entrancements and engagements with *being* which arise in the multiple philosophical and theological systems of human thinking; *and* it is capable of delineating the unsystematic experiences of individuals and communities, their everyday, ordinary, earthed, embodied yearnings which many human beings do not, cannot or will not seek to offer a name.

However, I am perhaps defeated from the start. There are many who see it as the very stamp of their faith never to question their traditional, institutional or dogmatic belief system; never to compare their beliefs with other faith expressions. For them, such a huge and billowing umbrella as 'the sacred' does not make sense. It would involve entertaining the proximity of the *everyday* to the *sacred*. In other words, there are always those who experience a certainty in their faith based on exclusion of anything or anyone who does not adhere to their own rock-solid belief system. This approach can think of the sacred only in elevated, authoritative, hierarchical or exclusionary terms.

But 'the sacred' as a category has dimensions which open up, reaching back in history towards the so-called primitive and often blood-soaked rituals of our forebears, and moving forward into the current moment. We recognise that ancient and contemporary worlds are acquainted with their full share of religious bloodiness, factionalism and war: Afghanistan, Pakistan and the Taliban; Israel and Palestine; Liberal against conservative Christian in the USA; continuing imperialism in regard to Indigenous peoples' belief systems and practices. Yet this essay argues that as we enter the so-called post-religious era (for some a hopeful descriptor, but not a highly factual one given the palpable reality of religions, take them or leave them, in the world today) there have never been more green shoots sprouting around the possibilities of sacredness.

I see these shoots growing in the cracks and fissures of war zones, around old temples and churches, and in, for some, the most counter intuitive of places in Western culture: contemporary music; the environmental movement; the voices of Indigenous peoples and their honouring of the land and ancestors; in the banalities and witticisms of advertising; in film and graffiti. This pervasiveness can be viewed with hope. It is a hope that the sacred yearnings of humanity are capable of slipping the traces of mere violence, as well as the strangulation by systemic or institutional rigidity, and that they such yearnings blossom through all human experience.

However, for Mark C Taylor, Professor of Religious Studies at Columbia University, America, there seems to be less hope, and more gloom involved in these eruptions of what he calls religion in the contemporary world. Writing in the American context, Taylor writes:

> You cannot understand the world today if you do not understand religion. Never before has religion been so powerful and so dangerous. No longer confined to church, synagogue, and mosque, religion has taken to the streets by filling airways and networks with images and messages that create fatal conflicts, which threaten to rage out of control.[1]

Confronted by the bloodshed and ongoing aggression spawned in the name of religion, many would agree with Taylor. But it is significant that he is using that word *religion* here. In America there is a very different environment and set of vocabularies around the category of the sacred from what we find in Australia, I would argue. Taylor, uses the term *religion* to cover the plethora of phenomena which includes: God, divinity, institutional religion, the politics of religion, individual belief and unbelief, creativity, the numinous, transcendence, faith, hope, love, dogma, worship, justice, and so on. While we might all recognise Taylor's disheartening scenario, is there room for more hope in the pervasiveness of the sacred both here in contemporary Australia and elsewhere? Do we—or might we—deploy a different vocabulary, and the fresh thinking that can go with it, a vocabulary which does not forget the violence of the sacred, but remembers also the human hopes and endeavours which are embraced by it?

At first blush we might answer this question decisively in the negative: is a new vocabulary, a sense of hope, possible even in laconic, secular, disenchanted Australia? A well-worn discourse decrees Australia to be particularly barren in terms of the sacred. Australian historian of the colonial period Alan Grocott argues that 'The typical bushman did not "care a fig" for theology, heaven or hell, or any of the consolations of the Christian religion; he was far more concerned with the pleasures of the flesh. His strength and comfort came from mateship'.[2] Arriving as a missionary to NSW in May 1818, aboard the convict transport Lady Castlereagh, young

1. Mark C Taylor, *After God* (Chicago: University of Chicago Press, 2007), 1.
2. Cited in Robert L Gallagher, '"Me and God, we'd be Mates": Towards an Aussie Contextualised Gospel', in *International Bulletin of Missionary Research*, July 1, 2006, at <www.highbeam.com/doc/1G1-148479941.html>. Accessed 5 November 2009.

Methodist minister, the Reverend Walter Lawry must have had quite a personal crossing! Lawry wrote in his journal upon arrival: 'Every kind of immorality prevails amongst the infidel part of the colony, but I think often, that it is not more abundant than either London or Portsmouth.'[3] It would actually have taken a generous and open imagination for a young Methodist clergyman in 1818 to understand both the degradations and the common human threads visible in colonial NSW and Regency England.

There are of course a wealth of differing characterisations about Australians and the sacred. Gary Bouma's recent work *Australian Soul*, echoing Manning Clark, describes Australians as possessing 'a serious quiet reverence, a deliberate silence . . . an inarticulate awe and a serious distaste for glib wordiness'.[4] This description comes closer to my own sense of the unspoken aspect of many Australians' contemplation of the sacred. However, all of these commentators, I would argue, are looking broadly, even monolithically, at a still colonial, European, Christian Australia. It can not be said that the new communities of refugees and migrants from Catholic, Moslem and Buddhist homelands share these same kinds of shy, inarticulate bushman attitudes from the era of Henry Lawson and Banjo Patterson.

So where does the choice of the word 'sacred', and the claim that the contemporary sacred is a pervasive category, lead us? The argument of this book is that what is needed now, globally, is a spirit and an approach which apprehend sacredness as alive in multiple ways, beyond what Taylor and others have decried as the power and the constrictions of institutional religion. Again, Taylor is cautious and often gloomy about the wrong-headedness of *religious* pervasiveness. He writes:

> An important phenomenon now that has not received adequate attention is the sophisticated use of media by the religious right in this country. Conservative Protestants are always far ahead of others in their use of media. The reason for this goes back to the Protestant reformers for whom the primary mission was spreading the Word of God. The technology then was print. Today the heirs of this tradition have extraordinarily sophisticated media networks—not just television but books, music CDs, videos, even video games

3. W Lawry to WMMC (World Methodist Missionary Committee), September 1818, AJCP, M124.
4. Cited in Paul Collins, 'Australians Quietly Spiritual', in *Eureka Street*, 17/8 (2007), at <www.eurekastreet.com.au>. Accessed 10 November 2009.

> . . . To understand the role of religion in today's world involves understanding that kind of use of media.[5]

Of course religion does indeed allow and actively produce these kinds of manipulations and oppositions, albeit in the name of embracing humanity. But what of the less systematic, often more spontaneous or ephemeral manifestations of the sacred that arise—are created, drawn upon, dreamed up—in popular and artistic cultures? Sacredness has burst out everywhere, and no one group has media rights. Sacredness is in the eye of beholders, and receivers, and unbelievers; it is in our face in popular music, film, political debates, literature, music; it is at ANZAC day gatherings, Sorry Days and Bridge crossings, and yes, even at the football. It is on advertising billboards and in graffiti. Yearning for sacred meaning manifests itself—yes, even in the 'godless' capitalist Western world—as the place where our deepest fears, angers, dreams, hopes, doubts, longings, joys are brought into relief, either individually or communally. And the responses to these manifestations are multiple too. They can produce silence where there has been a chaos of words; or language after repressed silence. They may—and often do—provoke anger, or wonder, or self-questioning, or questioning of others' actions. It is possible to think of this pervasiveness as the action of God's Spirit, or the Holy Spirit. Young boys of twelve might not call it this, but they do locate a sense of awe and hope and joy and despair in their football team's ups and downs. As do some fifty-nine year olds of my acquaintance! Can we accept that in so many popular manifestations of human culture a sacred human yearning links us together? It is perhaps in our attitudes and responses to others, as they participate in culture, that the parameters of the sacred are being formed and reformed. So if we can, at least for the space of this argument, stretch and adapt our idea of 'sacredness' so that it touches the everyday, material, ephemeral, unsystematic, often boisterous lives of others, we might ask: how pervasive is the sacred in everyday cultures?

I woke one morning recently in Northcote, the suburb of Melbourne, Australia in which I have lived for twenty-fve years, and outside my door was 'Heaven' (figure 1).

5. Mark C Taylor, in interview at <www.columbia.edu/cu/news/08/01/taylor html>. Accessed 18 November 2009.

Figure 1: Heaven outside my door, Northcote Victoria, 2009.

The old khaki green bus was dilapidated, and what you might consider an eyesore. It carried everything on its back—bikes, basins, rugs, and multiple large containers for petrol or water. Inside was crammed with more stuff. I saw only one inhabitant of the bus, a guy in his early forties, pretty much a latter day hippy with long hair, ragged, homespun clothes, and a proficient air, as he set up 'camp' in our street. Around him he gathered a range of (largely unspoken) responses from his new neighbours. Mostly it was a silent politeness, laced with repressed concerns voiced amongst each other: how long would he be here, where did he go to the toilet, how did he cook, did he have council approval to park in our street? No-one commented on the fact that the bus was called 'Heaven', its name clearly sign-posted on the destination panel at the front of the bus. It's name was, of course, ironic, even funny, wasn't it? Or perhaps it was making an *unironic* statement to all the middle-class mortgagees in the street about the freedom of getting about in a bus called heaven.

'Looks more like Hell to me', grumbled Pete down the street.
'I wonder if the Council knows', said Bert from number thirteen.

I found my neighbours' responses ranged from passive aggression, to open irritation, to concern for the safety of young daughters. But generally no-one took any action. The bus disappeared after about two weeks, and I missed it. I also regretted not having made contact, not even having said hello at least, and passing a few moments conversation with Heaven's driver. I was curious about the child's bike included on the roof rack; I wanted to see myself—to be—more than the slightly stiff-lipped neighbour in the bourgeois house. Heaven has come back, a couple of times, and gone away again. It has parked in different spots down the street, perhaps out of deference for the various owners. But I have never actually got to speak to the man in the bus.

This strange little un/suburban moment has continued to prod at me. I find humour in the naming of the bus. For me, the bus has been, in its odd, ramshackle presence, a welcome incursion into the polite normalities and policed ways of suburban behaving. Here is someone—sad, homeless, quite content, rudely un-suburban, I do not know—randomly coming into the neat spaces of our everyday, making me think. Disturbing my equilibrium just a little; certainly asking me how I am. How I relate to someone from 'outside'. Does this scenario impinge on the sacred? To answer that, I might choose to hop on a moral wagon and castigate the busman in roundly self-righteous terms: he is breaking the law; he is dirty; he is transient; he does not act gratefully for the space we have afforded him. Alternatively, I might question myself about the appropriateness or adequacy or openness of my responses, and those of my neighbours. But the bus called Heaven, in its randomness, its signs of human vulnerability, and its surprisingness, prompts me to ask myself how ready or capable I am of stepping beyond the borders of habit, stock response, fear, suspicion, or a sense of the hierarchies of council permits, rate-paying tidiness, ownership. How rigidified have I become, how soldered into the rightness of my own way of being?

The bus reminds me of the iconic scene in the 1999 Sam Mendes film *American Beauty*, where the vulnerable young man stands distracted, almost outside of time—entranced by the beauty of the wind turning a plastic bag round and round in small, graceful circles. There is a spontaneity and enchantment in the scene at what is untidy, not arranged, expected, needed or manipulable. Perhaps the pervasiveness of the sacred acts like this: it asks us to be open enough to embrace such moments, or experiences; it nudges us out of our scheduled and law-ridden worlds. It promises to reveal the limits of our own impacted certainties. It is important, too, to remember that the supermarket chain Sainsbury's very quickly ripped off this scene from *American Beauty* for its advertising needs. Nothing lasts forever.

Graffiti also acts as this kind of breaker of limits. It irritates many because it is usually illegal, messy, created by adolescents or would-be adolescents. It desecrates privately owned property. For others, it can be the expression of freedom, anti-capitalist, a random kind of beauty, an open-ended message. Often on trips around my suburb I see my favourite piece of graffiti, the angel (figure 2). She is unusual in the world of graffiti, as she's been there for over five years, on a concrete wall four metres wide by three metres high, primitivist in style. Her gaze is implacable, her lips full and sensuous, her hair shaggy, her wings feathered, textured. She (or so I have dubbed her) arrests me whenever I see her.

Figure 2. The angel on the south wall, the old Fitzroy football oval, Freeman St. Fitzroy, Melbourne.

Figure 3: Detail of the angel on the south wall.

What can we say about this kind of intervention into the suburban landscape? How do the neighbours along the opposite side of the road feel, in their gentrified—and now very expensive—inner urban houses built in the late nineteenth century? For them, does the angel send a shiver of awareness, intimations of another dimension, or an other dimension *within* this concrete, prosaic, lived-in city street? Each viewer of the angel will have their own way of deciding what that other dimension might be, or in fact whether that *is* indeed their response. Some will simply be annoyed at the graffiti. The angel doesn't preach, or set up rules, or insist on anything. Perhaps that's why she might annoy some and enchant others. But she is a presence—temporary, primitive, weathered, ethereal, vulnerable—in her urban, scribbled condition. She might be the starting point of conversations. A tiny filament of imaginative response—knowing or unknowing, educated or spontaneous—to sacred possibilities.

One objection to graffiti, and to other popular, earthed, palpable manifestations of sacred concepts or characters, is that they undermine or misrepresent the transcendent nature of (some people's) divinity. For early Protestants, and some latter-day ones, there is to be no graven image, no ornamentation of truths that are seen to exist *beyond* human imagination. Except of course for the bible, which converts the 'word' in 'word of God' into a different kind of icon, the Logos: the never-to-be replicated, but only to be repeated Word of God. All other human words are in the service of This Word. This to me is a strange, hollowed out understanding of the beauties and travails of the lived, fleshed world. It seems that stemming from this—shall we call it puritan—notion of the human world, the sacred can only be inadequately (or worse, blasphemously) represented here and now.

Refusal of any graven image is different, but related to, Buddhist understandings of the place of the phenomenal. The middle road of Western Buddhism offers, through the practices of meditation, different modes of comprehending the place of the material world in the journey towards enlightenment. In his 1906, often reprinted volume *Zen for Americans*, Soyen Shaku set about to do just as his title indicates, to make comprehensible to an already capitalist-directed America a different set of relations between the physical and the metaphysical. Early in his volume he provides a well-known saying of Buddhists:

> The Buddha-Body fills the world,
> Being immanent universally in all things,
> It will make itself manifest wherever and whenever conditions are matured,
> Though it never leaves this Seat of Bodhi[6]

In order to explain the relationship of earthly to transcendent realities in this gâthâ, Shaku continues:

> . . . the idea of sameness is rather dogmatically expressed: 'The Buddha-Body fills the world.' In this the content of sameness is called Buddha-Body or in Sanskrit Buddhakâya. The Buddhakâya, which is also often called Dharmakâya, is the reason, life, and norm of all particular existences. When we penetrate through the diversity of all these individual phenomena, we encounter everywhere this indwelling Body and therein find the unity or sameness (*samatâ*) of things.
>
> The principle of diversity is declared in the second line of the gâthâ, which makes the Buddha-Body universally immanent in all things. The Buddha-Body, the essence of existence, though absolutely one

6. Soyen Shaku, *Zen for Americans,* translated by DT Suzuki (La Salle, Illinois: Open Court Publishing: 1906/2003).

> in itself, allows itself to be diversified as the lilies of the field, as the fowls of the air, as the creatures of the water, or as the inhabitants of the woods. For it is in the inherent nature of the Buddha-Body that it individualizes itself in the manifoldness of the phenomenal world. It does not stand alone outside particular existences, but it abides in them and animates them and makes them move freely. By thus abandoning its absolute transcendentality, it has subjected itself to certain conditions such as space, time, and causation. Its essence is infinite, but its manifestations are finite and limited.[7]

This influential explanation of the Buddhist principles of unity, diversity and immanence in the relationship of the phenomenal to the transcendent carries with it a deep sense of the pervasiveness of the sacred. It offers an account of both the universal and the individual that challenges so many fundamentalist understandings of sacred and profane as mutually exclusive categories. What we read here does not yet establish the ethical and meditative implications of such holistic thinking, but it begins to point to some of those implications, especially in regard to the vision and discipline necessary to apprehend the sacred within the earthed.

Christianity and Islam have, of course, their different histories of such relations. Yet the questions, I would venture to argue, are the same: how do earthed, fleshed, mortal and sensuous beings apprehend the spiritual? And how do such understandings inform human practices and ethical decisions? Examining the history of the painful and tortuous religious separations of the earthly and the transcendent would take us down many a rough and precipitous road. Here is one moment in such a journey, diverging as it does into many pathways, byways and cul de sacs:

In October, 1997 Andres Serrano's painting, 'Piss Christ' was being exhibited at the National Gallery of Australia in Melbourne. Catholic Archbishop George Pell unsuccessfully sought a Supreme Court injunction to ban public display of the work; two physical attacks were made on the painting, and the Gallery Director peremptorily removed it from public access. What was at stake here, in the passionate debate circling around a misty yellow depiction of the crucifixion of Jesus by an avant-garde artist from New York? For Pell and others, the work was declared blasphemous; it was the very opposite of their religious understandings of divinity. For others it opened out, in dramatic and immediate ways, the humanity of Jesus. But while the Christ came in human form, according to incarnation-

7. *Ibid*, 65–66.

ists, what has God got to do with urine? With human bodily functions? Supporters of the painting argued that it raised, in immediate and earthy ways, the realities of the incarnate God. For theologian Damien Casey the furore around 'Piss Christ' points to the nature of tolerance and openness to others, within the church and beyond:

> The claim that *Piss Christ* is offensive to Christians seems to suggest, incorrectly I believe, that *Piss Christ* has neither place nor precedent within the Christian tradition. To the extent that *Piss Christ* questions the boundaries between the sacred and the profane, it enacts what it represents. It threatens the identity of conservative Christians who respond by seeking to exclude it from the public realm. I consider that what is at stake is not merely the question of tolerance within a pluralist society but also that of tolerance within a pluralist Church. To whom do religious symbols belong and who has the authority to prescribe the manner in which they are used?[8]

I want to embrace wholeheartedly the spirit of Casey's argument here. However, the word 'tolerance' seems a little gentle in this case.

What is at stake, I believe, is not just tolerance, but the *rights* of groups and individuals to approach *any* representations of the sacred fearlessly and with open, questioning minds and hearts. This openness is an ideal, but it is a crucial beginning point too, in my larger argument about the pervasiveness of the sacred. As Casey asserts more strongly later in his essay, in relation to the nature of human involvement with sacred representations of all kinds

> . . . the concept of divine sovereignty as divine mastery over the world must be abandoned. God's place is with the abject every bit as much as it is on the high altar of the cathedral. Yes, the crucifix as a triumphant symbol is a delicious irony in keeping with the spirit of the gospels. But that irony is lost when we forget its strong association with both ignominy and abjection. Then it merely becomes a sign of domination.

Casey's question is: who has the right to dictate the scope of the sacred, and of sacred symbols abroad in culture? Church and government hier-

8. Damien Casey, 'Law & The Sacred: Sacrifice, Piss Christ, and Liberal Excess', in *Law, Text, Culture*, June (2000): 19.

archies often believe they have that paternalistic right, but a basic understanding of this present essay is that there is no need to approach sacred issues in fear, or censorship, or a fixed idea of what is sacred and what is profane. One bleeds into the other; the borders are transgressed and have been in multiple ways across the centuries, as human beings make meaning, sometimes casually, sometimes with intent. Surely it is in the to and fro of communication that meaning is processed and reprocessed. Sometimes these processes are laconic and ephemeral, sometimes passionate and long-remembered. But in all such pervasive manifestations of the sacred it is surely the manner in which we permit the rights of others to apprehend the multiple possibilities of the sacred that is central. To make choices and judgements which may alter across time; to debate, consider and be effected by all kinds of cultural and intellectual forms is part of being human. There is a dignity in every attempt, even those we might personally think misguided or imprecise or even evil.

I personally do not like the fervent fundamentalism I see in the billboard placed in a wheat field on Interstate 70 near Colby, Kansas in 2009 (figure 4). The brief account in *mxNews* reports:

> A painting of Jesus plonked in the middle of a wheat field sits on the roadside . . . Colby developers Tuffy and Linda Kay Taylor erected the painting as a comfort for motorists who travel down Interstate 70 at all hours of the day and night.[9]

Figure 4: Christ in the Wheatfield, Colby, Kansas, 2009.

9. 'The Wheat shall inherit the earth', in *mxNews*, Tuesday, July 21, (2009): 6. (Picture copyright AP. Posted by blogger Karen Graber,7.20 p.m., 11/5 on nbcactionnews.com).

From my perspective the vision rising up unexpectedly from the fields at tired travellers is almost comic. For me, this is partly because of the assumption that such a vision will be a comfort to all, rather than a threat, or a joke: an oversized Jesus, resplendent in first century style, atop a billboard. But it is also understandable that the billboard *might* be a comfort to many, and I would not want the developers, Tuffy and Linda Taylor, to be stripped of their right to erect such a sign. I am not impoverished by their action. I would, however, want to talk about the assumptions—emotional, intellectual and spiritual—behind their action, and the possible readings of the billboard. But that means that as a sign the Colby billboard is alive, and has effects that might be productive.

Similarly, how do we consider the conjunction of the sacred with popular culture in the mass outpourings of grief and loss, together with the temporary shrines set up in cities around the world, when Michael Jackson died? These shrines were made from pictures of Jackson, many flowers, and lots of scribbled messages. Notes left at the shrine in Madrid praised his musical genius, of course, but they also declared: 'Michael, you are my god'; 'Jacko is bigger than god'; 'All my prayers are with you Michael, as you walk on the moon.'

Figure 5: 'You are my personal God, I love you':
Makeshift Michael Jackson shrine, Christopher Columbus Place, Madrid, 2009.

In London, outside the Trocadero, Leicester Square, hundreds of messages declared that Jackson was supreme, and that he is now where he belongs, with the angels.

Figures 6–8: "Moonwalk your way to heaven":
The Michael Jackson shrine outside the Trocadero, London, 2009.

As we saw with the sudden death of Princess Diana, beauty, talent and fame sometimes coalesce in popular culture into something altogether bigger: an iconic and unstoppable expression of people's adoration, praise and grief. Of course not all the messages at these shrines were religious in nature, but they all expressed a powerful sense of mortal limits: the double realisation that human life can produce such unique (and often troubled, eccentric) achievements, together with mass sorrow at such human loss. An ontologically resonant moment rises up from people across national, ethnic, age and religious differences. It is a space in which all passionate fans, and many others, realise the depth of human ability and impressiveness (with a lot of media hype accompanying, of course), but also its limits. There is something—death—that is not controlled by human pride or achievement. Does such an unswerving fact point to a force beyond the human, a sacred force? Or is it a natural expression of animal being? Or both? Such moments are spaces in which all of us might communicate about the fragile limits of human power and mortality, and share our hopes or doubts about what might be beyond.

Such temporary shrines can be seen along highways and roadways everywhere. They proliferated after 9/11 at corners and light poles, and along the fences surrounding the place where the Trades Centre Towers had stood. And on the steps of State buildings after the Bali terrorist bombings in 2002 (see chapter 2 on postmodern rituals). And many of us erect temporary and sometimes more permanent markers—a tree, a cross, the sign of the crescent moon, a cairn of stones, a fading photograph, an elaborate headstone or mausoleum—when those who mean something in our lives—a lover, a wife, a friend, a child, our pets, our compatriots—have died. Such tributes and shrines can be moving in their expression of loss, and they can also be chilling in their anger and promises of revenge for such loss. But in their profoundly human responses to the limits of the human, do they point us to sacred dimensions?

Are there still prophetic words to be heard today? When the apocalyptically prophetic words of Al Qaeda are heard, the cosmopolitan west sometimes smirks at such quasi-biblical, desert-dwelling pronouncements. But it also cowers, afraid in the presence of terrorist might. And then there are the military responses by many western nations. Such responses are sometimes voiced directly in terms of God and right, but more often in terms of the defence of democracy. Democracy, supposedly the people's might, stands as a metonym for righteousness, civilisation, and for many, Christianity opposed to Islam, especially in the American context.

At the same time, another kind of democracy takes the guise of individualist freedom, and is exercised by the artists—street and main stage—in this hyper-mediated era. In songs, and on walls, in poetry and painting, in the expressions of fandom and celebrity, there is an ongoing stream of meaning making: images of beauty and confronting violence, of ephemeral and more lasting significance. In each generation, each decade, each year of each generation, the forms, the language and the focus of such meaning-making is changed by human desire to communicate *where and how* the potential for meaning might be. In the environmental movement, in the embracing of 'foreign' religious traditions such as Buddhism and Hinduism by Western people, and in artistic production, human beings voice their fears that there may not be ultimate meaning; and they voice their hope. This is not to argue that all such strivings amount to the same single meaning. Of course they don't. But it is the same pervasive desire to wrestle with the deepest experiences and longings of human existence that motivates such strivings. Around this absent centre, the sacred, we make fools of ourselves; we become a suicide bomber or a peace activist; we listen to the Dali Lama, open our ears and our minds to consider one prophet or another. How foolish and how beautiful, this human, sacred longing. We turn our face to the lovely, vanishing natural world, or we write poetry; we paint 'Piss Christ' and yes, even rail against it, because we want to participate in profound and shaping ideas and emotions. So often this desire leads to violence, to mass persuasion and to national self-righteousness. But if we can open ourselves to the turbulent stream of sacred meaning-making—refusing to be impatient, all-knowing, dogmatic—then we have the possibility of truly listening to one another in a process of discernment and mutual dignity. Such hopes are perhaps utopian, and always in danger of failure, but they are also what impels the human spirit as it seeks to sift and weigh, celebrate and discern what is sacred.

One blog contributor to 'Songfacts', Alexandria Conrad, responding to discussion of the Simon and Garfunkel song 'Sounds of Silence' expresses her love of the lyrics, at the same time as she registers what she considers to be the mis-readings that surround the song:

> . . . 'the writing of the prophets is written on the subway walls and tenement halls' . . . seems to be a statement that decency and honesty is rarely if ever presented through our PR and Politically Correct obsessive media—lying politicians, advertisements, slanted journalism, etc. The sentiments of the 'everyman' to or perhaps the proletariat are of greater value because they lack the ulterior motive of tv anchormans and such—further, they are not as removed. prophets have almost as a tradition not sat in the seats of statesmen. the words are ignored, however well written insightful or prophetic, by your average passerby. That the song is in part about

> the difficulty of communication or at least meaningful communication among mankind is no surprise to me (though I believe there may be more to it). I also feel that as there is a great deal of biblical symbolism that their supposed feux pas of saying 'hear my words that I might teach you' was in part an allusion to prophetic teachings—presumptuous or not it is hard to say, though i would not fault them for that any more than i would fault nietzche for writing thus spake zarathustra in imitation of the biblical style - - - IT WAS FOR ARTISTIC AFFECT!!![10]

There are many aspects of this contribution that fascinate me. The contributor, a self-declared non-religious person, is intrigued by truth-telling, prophecy, symbolism and teachings. She also seems open to these sacred techniques, and to their manifestations in a popular song. She has her own hierarchy of potential truth sources, with poetic nuance and symbolism at the top and 'tv anchormans', PR and advertising men, journalists and 'statesmen' at the bottom. And she is both wary and open to prophetic voices. But here she is, blogging about something that moves her and opens her up to 'the difficulty of communication or at least meaningful communication', and to the ways a song, shared by several generations, can turn us to the pervasiveness of prophetic or truth-bearing claims. The blogger here does not necessarily *believe* in any structure or institution of meaning, but she wants to contribute passionately to the discussion about meaning. She is savvy about the cultural codes and modes—biblical style, prophetic teaching, presumptuous claims to truth—and she wades in, boots and all. She exudes that living, breathing desire to communicate, and meaningfully.

As Obama enters the second year of his Presidency of the United States, Americans and many other peoples around the world have before them a man with high rhetorical skills and competencies. His techniques of persuasion and directness are prophetic in their nuances and in their poetic power, and they are also connected to powerfully transformative political undertakings such as Health Care in the USA This may mean that he is nothing more or less than a consummate politician. In Australia too, we have a Prime Minister, Kevin Rudd, who speaks of the profound influence on him of Dietrich Bonhoeffer, the Christian martyr who died seeking justice in Nazi Germany. This is the Prime Minister who brought

10. Conrad, Alexandria, VA, *Songfacts*, at <www.songfacts.com/detail.php?id=796>. Accessed November 15 2009.

us the two powerfully symbolic national Sorry days: for Indigenous Australians, and for the forgotten Australians, children abused in orphanages after the Second World War and since. In doing so, Rudd taps into deep psychic streams in Australian history. But again, he is for some nothing more or less than a cunning politician. And charisma is awash in the current leaderships of France, Russia and Italy, in the very different figures of Sarkozy, Putin and Berlusconi. The polis does not trust mere political charisma, but they are also drawn to it. Our secular political structures are what we have. We enter into them at various levels and varying measures of doubt and hope. We criticise and we vote (or not). In all this we express our desires for something better, more just, truer, more hopeful, more constructive and humane, more visionary of a future we can live in. These desires are not separate from the desire for sacred meaning. We might not use that word, especially if it carries connotations of religiosity and dogmatism with it. But if we participate—if we have the privilege and freedom to participate, politically, sacramentally, artistically, scientifically—then we place ourselves in the role of meaning-makers. Just how open, questioning, believing or sceptical are we, along the changing and temporary points of our participation in this meaning-making? My argument has been that the pervasiveness of the sacred requires of us an openness which itself reflects the nature of the sacred. It is an openness that is under pressure at every point in the media-driven, militaristic, nationalistic and capitalist world. But it is also an openness that can and does flower in the multitude of surprising and unexpected cultural forms of the sacred, as we broker them together.

One of my PhD students is researching the impact of Buddhism in the contemporary West. His sense of the sacred is alive to the pervasiveness and the openness I have been arguing for, and should be given the final word:

> Sacredness unveils itself when we embrace all of our experience—from the heights of ecstasy to the depths of despondency—with non-grasping attentiveness; it is the breath of equanimity that awakens us to what is otherwise, unthinkable, impossible, unconditioned: the not-me, not-I, not-mine.

Works Cited

Brown, Pam. 'Pique', *50–50,* (Adelaide: Little Esther Books, 1997), 67–70.

Casey, Damien. 'Law & The Sacred: Sacrifice, Piss Christ, and Liberal Excess', in *Law, Text, Culture*, June (2000): 19.

Collins, Paul. 'Australians Quietly Spiritual', in *Eureka Street*, 17/8 (2007), at <www.eurekastreet.com.au>. Accessed 10 November 2009.

Conrad, Alexandria, *Songfacts*, at <www.songfacts.com/detail.php?id=796>. Accessed November 15 2009.

Gallagher, Robert, L. '"Me and God, we'd be Mates": Towards an Aussie Contextualised Gospel', in *International Bulletin of Missionary Research*, July 1, 2006, at <www.highbeam.com/doc/1G1-148479941.html>. Accessed 5 November 2009.

Gordon, Jenkins and Simon, Paul. 'The Sounds of Silence', MCA Music Publishing, 1965

Shaku, Soyen. *Zen for Americans,* translated by DT Suzuki (La Salle, Illinois: Open Court Publishing: 1906/2003).

Taylor, Mark C. *After God* (Chicago: University of Chicago Press, 2007), 1.
---, interview at <www.columbia.edu/cu/news/08/01/taylor.html>. Accessed 18 November 2009.

'The Wheat shall inherit the earth', in *mxNews*, Tuesday, July 21, (2009): 6.

Chapter One

Popular Cultures/Sacredness

A huge billboard faces me as I crawl down perpetually jammed Punt Road in Melbourne. The billboard's wild purple and yellow-daubed sports fan (male) leer over the northbound traffic. The message: 'Sport is a Religion, so pray for Yamaha Stadium Sound.' Canny advertising, hooking into aussie culture, selecting an aussie take on religion/sport (fun, serious, primitive, fanatic, central). Next, there's the *Next* fashion ad, with its larger than life photograph of a gorgeously dressed young female eying off the pope's long white robe, comparing outfits. Fashion as religion, or better than, really, is the inference—she looks mildly amused, and he looks a little nonplussed. And then there are the many Qantas advertisements for 'Spirit of Australia' featuring Aboriginal figures, with backdrops of Uluru and the red desert. As cultural tour businesses know, there's money to be made in taking urban, non-indigenous tourists to visit their 'spiritual other', the Aboriginal.[1] Or there's the multicultural, children's version of the ad, with all the little global travellers of the future featured in wonderful locations. Spirit of Australia.

As an observer participant of Australian popular culture, and as an observer participant of religion, I am asking a postmodern question: how do I read the plethora of phenomena—advertisements, soapies, pop songs,

1. See firstly the Central Land Council, Pitjantjatjara Council and the Mutitjulu Community, *Sharing the Park: Anangu Initiatives in Ayres Rock Tourism* (Alice Springs: Institute for Aboriginal Development, 1991), for discussion of the claims of tourism on Aboriginal sacred sites. Secondly, a range of important academic essays and volumes have been written about these competing claims: David Tacey, *Edge of the Sacred: Transformation in Australia* (North Blackburn: HarperCollins, 1995). Barry Hill, *The Rock: Travelling to Uluru* (Sydney: Allen & Unwin, 1994); Julie Marcus, 'The Journey out to the Centre: the cultural appropriation of Ayers Rock', in Cowlishaw, Gillian (Editor); Morris, Barry (Editor). *Race Matters: Indigenous Australians and 'Our' Society* (Canberra: Aboriginal Studies Press, 1997), 29–51.

self-help/spirituality groups and books—which at different levels employ religion, or religious figures, or more broadly, 'sacredness' (or its markers), in order to sell. This is not the question: 'should I read such phenomena?' because living in the postmodern world means I cannot help but take in to some extent the barrage of words, images and messages sent at me constantly. For some *religious* observers this is not worth thinking about, for they see such phenomena as mere secular flippancies. I guess we could call this the postmodern ostrich position (head buried, but arse still subject to the barrage). Or more seriously, others deride the capitalist, silly, pop culture jockeying to grasp at any thread of cultural signification in order to make a buck. A few might be even more aggrieved at the profanity of such usages. But the question remains for both the secular and the religious observer: do these flotsam and jetsam of popular Western culture have any significance beyond the ephemeral? Are they indicators of contemporary Western attitudes to religion, and to spirituality, and if so, what is being indicated? And further, what might our responses be to the fact of such usages—resistance, or seeing in them signs which need to be read, or even seeing them as *hopeful* indications of a spiritual hunger, or somewhere in between?[2]

In their wonderfully provocative volume *The Feminine and the Sacred* Catherine Clément and Julia Kristeva have published a series of (highly polished) letters to each other, circling around the question of the sacred. Along the way they offer a number of 'definitions' of sacredness, each of which takes into account the bodily, the everyday, sexuality and the material. Kristeva writes:

> What if the sacred were the unconscious perception the human being has of its untenable eroticism; always on the borderline between nature and culture, the animalistic and the verbal, the sensible and the nameable? What if the sacred were not the religious need for protection and omnipotence that institutions exploit but the jouissance of that cleavage—of that power/powerlessness—of that exquisite lapse? This incompleteness is explored while revisiting, in one's mind, childhood, dependence, or a more or less strange, more or less 'telling' word.[3]

2. See Meaghan Morris, 'Banality in Cultural Studies', in *Logics of Television: Essays in Cultural Criticism*, edited by Patricia Mellencamp (Bloomington: Indiana University Press), 14–43, for a theoretical discussion of different reader positions in response to popular culture.
3. Catherine Clément, and Julia Kristeva, *The Feminine and the Sacred*, translated by Jane Marie Todd (Palgrave: Columbia University Press, 2001), 27.

We in 'the West' are constantly bathed by this flood of popular cultural 'jouissance', continuously, often painfully, made aware of our animal, material, sexual, bodily selves. But at the same time, as postmoderns we are teased, through the very same media, with the ephemerality of the individual phenomenon, to acknowledge the simulation, the rush of simulacra, the merely representational nature of what we see and hear and taste. So, we are offered more 'reality'—more 'body', 'sensation', 'pleasure', 'satisfaction'—*and* we understand the transience of such offers. Of course, this double whammy does not necessarily lead to an apprehension of 'the sacred', let alone a definition, but in the process of probing this gap there is a search going on. To block out the flood of the everyday world, its changing cultural forms, would be equivalent to prematurely closing off questions about this 'untenable eroticism', this cleavage, this intuition or awareness of our power/powerlessness. And obviously many millions of Western viewers and consumers are not blocking out the flood. Some might say we are wallowing in it, though at the same time we 'can't get enough of it'. Others might say that such wallowing is a desperate avoidance of the eternal. Approaches to the sacred are shaped, often, by the extent to which the partial, human and processual nature of 'the way' is celebrated; and, in counterpoint, the extent to which the sacred is envisaged as a state: the eternal, the unchanging, the serene.

The most recent edition of *Continuum*, the journal of that fairly brash and border-slashing academic discipline Media and Cultural Studies[4] is entitled *Serenity Now!* The title is a quote from television's *Seinfeld* character George Costanza's father, who screams this demand 'with the fury of an expletive rather than the calm of a meditation technique'.[5] Editors of this volume, Wendy Parkins and Tara Brabazon from Murdoch University, have gathered together a range of essays on what they refer to variously as 'technologies of self', 'structures of feeling', self-help and spirituality. Topics range from *Oprah* and other self-help television shows, to Native American spirituality, to spiritual/sexual workshops and reading, to the eco-spiritual capitalism of The Body Shop. For most of the authors in the volume 'spiritual beliefs and practices are simultaneously (and paradoxically) embedded in everyday life'.[6] Whether it is self-help groups, television shows or reading, transformation is the bottom line in the collection,

4. *Continuum: Journal of Media and Cultural Studies*, 15/2 (July 2001), Wendy Parkins and Tara Brabazon, editors.
5. Parkins and Brabazon, 141.
6. Parkins and Brabazon, 142.

'transformation of subjects and the often mundane and domestic spaces in which they are situated'.[7] There's a lot to be learnt in this volume, particularly when we return to that methodological/epistemological question about whether popular culture can be an indicator of current attitudes to religion and to the sacred. These cultural studies scholars do not want to be mere observers. They are inevitably embedded and embroiled in the culture they are analysing; they are awake to the everyday and quotidian (temporary) resting places of the sacred; and they are willing to laugh at others and themselves as they wrestle with the contiguity of the mundane and the transcendent. Transformation of self and community is the recurring focus, even as that desire is lampooned for the crassness of its vehicles and the rapidity and fashion-frenzied nature of change.

So if you are a connoisseur of high culture only, and disdain the suggestion that popular culture has any relationship to sacredness, stop reading now, if you haven't already. What are the popular culture vehicles—in which most of Western and many parts of Asian, African and South American cultures partake—driving many of us today? First, Film. That magical medium, shape-changing and transformatory, has become the standard ride for millions of consumers. The current $US80 million Paramount Pictures blockbuster *Lara Croft: Tomb Raider* features the gloriously feminine and athletic shape of Lara, played by the sumptuous Angelina Jolie displaying her astonishing physical prowess across the screen. But Lara needs to 'come home', and in a scene depicting the orphaned millionairess sitting submissive and meditative at the feet of her Cambodian Buddhist monk/mentor we are presented with the moment when tough, sexy, rich young woman reveals need for sacred—for an oasis of peace, gentleness, healing and focus—and of course a lost father figure. The monk touches her wounded arm, which magically and instantly heals, and then sends her on her way with assurances that purity of mind and adherence to Buddhist beliefs will bring ultimate victory in the battle against the bad guys (and they are guys) which lies ahead: the sacred as primal (in its exoticised ancient jungle, third world setting), magical (instantaneous and miraculous) and feminine, pretty much for the girl who already has everything—looks, strength, money and verve. How do we read this small but significant dose of sacredness here? It could well be read as a comfortable and one might say *American* brand of commodity religion, heavily into achievement and self-actualisation. For the woman who has every-

7. Parkins and Brabazon, 142.

thing, this too shall be given. Or for *the man*—for example, Richard Gere and other megastars' allegiances to various social justice causes linked to Buddhist teachings and institutions. Of course it is not that we have the information—nor perhaps even the right—to know how committed and sincere these much-publicised adherents of Buddhism are, or what their theology might be. But we can, and I would argue we need to, ask *how the media depicts the commodity of religious belief.*

In the rock arena, figures such as Nick Cave, Marilyn Manson, Madonna and U2 engage in their visual presentations as well as in their lyrics, with the accoutrements of religion. Madonna's name, and that of her daughter Lourdes, as well as her brand of accessory crucifixes, have for two decades sold her as a postmod, Catholic Italian, freewheeling chick, a shape-changer who is seemingly able to adapt her dress, sexuality, morality and charisma endlessly. Countless academic articles have celebrated her shape-changing postmodernity, amongst which her religious affiliations count as but one attribute. Her recent marriage to Guy Richie, in his ancestral Scottish village—full church wedding, Lourdes as flower girl, multi-million dollar wedding breakfast, mega-star guest list—was for many a sumptuously postmodern religious spectacle. It was postmodern because it celebrated the limits of traditional and contemporary capitalist culture: bagpipes *and* the latest technologies, the family and the world stage, Presbyterianism and sumptuous aesthetics. Could a spectator make any attempt at moral or religious observation about such mediated spectacle? Some would argue that it is impossible to comment on, that there are too many layers of media between spectator and event. But in fact it is the spectacle itself, the fantasy it hooks into—untold fame, riches, happiness, and piety too—which is what so many read and digest. And against which so many would read their own little, more mundane lives, presumably.

On their new album, 'De Rigeurmortis',[8] off-beat Australian group TISM (This is Serious Mum) refers often to things religious, always two tongues in cheek. For example, in 'Honk If You Love Fred Durst' the lyrics are as follows:

> God looked at the spread sheets for Christianity
> 'We need more than product placement on R&B CDs
>
> Youth masses ain't workin', cut the Pope's budget back
> Get the youth demographic thinkin' Jesus ain't wack'

8. TISM, 'De Rigeurmortis', Mushroom Records, Australia, 2001.

'We need a teenage pop diva, a virgin sex-kitten
Carnal knowledge innuendo immaculate conception
Start a shrinking violet bedroom wannabe S Eleven
Be bad girls be nasty and you will get to heaven.'

Jesus rocks tha' mic.

For our next apostle we need to go for cred
Get a vegan greenie DJ with a shaven head
He can rip off some old bluesmen like a real techno vandal
But tell everybody he's unfit to tie my sandals.

It's time for the Messiah of Hardcore Christian Inc.
Son, reverse your baseball cap, jerk your arms like Lancelot Link
It's born-again stone phat bitch-ass boy fantasy religion
Feed the holy moshpit Limp Bizkit communion.

For the initiated, this hardcore parody of hardcore Fred Durst and his band Limp Bizkit is a perfect send up, and like all satires, it flaunts its own prowess about the subject matter, imitating the heavy guitar riffs and serious content of LimpBizkit, while adding a twee 'beep beep' voice-over on and around the chorus. These satirists are well acquainted with the zeitgeist of teen hard rock icons and concert going. They know the youth demographic, as well as the kind of cool Christian evangelism that wants to sell Jesus to pop culture. Their suggestions for a more hip Christian saleability, reflecting what of course already circulates, are 'virgin sex-kittens' (Mandy Moore, Britney Spears, the Atomic Kittens?), vegan greenie DJs, and a kind of moshpit salvation. Theirs is, in their own smartarse parlance, an 'immaculate conception'. It operates through a minefield of codes and satires of satires, both *within* pop culture and as an extension of it, through satire.

Still in the rock arena, the quite different out-workings, and the image and achievements of U2 headman Bono are fascinating. The lyrics of U2's songs have been variously political and spiritual—along with lots of love lyrics of course. Their extraordinary success as pop wizards has opened a range of big doors for Bono, whose recent work for Jubilee 2000, seeking to address questions of third world debt, has seen him in conference with world leaders, including Bill Clinton, the chair of the US Federal Reserve, Alan Greenspan, and the pope. The latter was reportedly given a pair of Bono's famous sunglasses in return for a set of the pope's beads. Various enormous amounts of money discounted from third world debt were attributed in the media to Bono's efforts.

Bono's fame has also led him into association with equally famous artists, such as his friendship and collaboration with Salman Rushdie. The lyrics to U2's recent song 'The ground beneath her feet' were written by Rushdie, and Rushdie's 1999 novel of the same name is about an Indian-born mega popstar, strung out somewhere between John Lennon, Bono and Rushdie himself, caught up in the rock world of drugs and gigantic consumption, and a spiritual need for a simpler, more ascetic life. Novels have since their inception in the eighteenth century been an arena in which large questions of secularity and sacredness have been constructed and addressed. Many critics have argued that the early eighteenth century novels of Defoe, Richardson and Sterne, and the Gothic writers such as Monk Lewis and Anne Radcliffe, for example, developed the novel in the context of the European enlightenment, as a place in which to advance secular, and often openly anti-religious polemics. Rushdie's postmodern fiction continues this tradition. From *Midnight's Children*, to *The Satanic Verses*, to the most recent *The Ground Beneath Her Feet* and *Fury*, Rushdie probes the parameters of this mighty novelistic struggle between religious and secular institutions and imaginations. In Rushdie these forces are most often nationalism, Islam, capitalism and consumerism, with both secular and religious forces running through them, sometimes indistinguishably, as Rushdie tracks in his high postmodern way, the intersections of secular and sacred. In chapter 12 of *The Ground Beneath Her Feet*, entitled 'Transformer', Ormus Cama, the cosmopolitan, touchingly innocent rock songwriter, describes to his beloved Vina his apocalyptic vision of that other place, 'the gash in the real', which he is experiencing on their flight on 'the red-eye to New York'.

> Imagine if this, he says, waving an arm, this, us, where we are, all of it, if it was all a movie on a screen and we were in it, a huge screen like at a drive-in or just hanging in space like a curtain, and then suppose there were slashes in the screen, a mad knifeman ran into the cinema and hacked at that curtain, so now there are these great rips going right across everything, across you, across the window, across the wing out there, across the stars, and you can see that behind the screen there's a whole other set of things going on, maybe another whole I doesn't know level, or maybe another movie screen with another movie playing, and there are people in that movie looking the other way through the rips and maybe seeing us.

> And beyond that movie another movie and another and another until who can guess.[9]

Not only does Rushdie use the symbols of the postmodern world, the cinema and film, space, flight, and madmen with knives, he uses them with humour and with high seriousness, often simultaneously. These are the tools of imagination for postmodern human beings, and they are used by Rushdie to depict the undepictable. Film and travel are both symbolic sites of transformation—in time, place, identity—that are most real to millions of postmodern consumers, so what else would he have his characters dream with? It is the frenzied actions of the mad knifeman, ripping the first curtain, which terrify, but which also begin to reveal the possibilities of that other place, the gash in the real which relativises all reals. The trauma at the base of this revelation is an ancient, recurrent and sacred trauma: where and how and for how long does my consciousness exist? Is the struggle towards understanding and full consciousness merely a fool's game, one tiny layer of repetitive activity in a universe, which merely mocks, and mirrors back the stupidity of the searcher? Is the mad knifeman our postmodern prophet, stabbing at the layers of unreality in a Baudrillardian revelation of surface and depth as one; all as screen hiding screen; actor and viewer inextricably mixed up?

The humour is in the racy excessiveness of Ormus' vision, in his listener/lover Vina's simultaneous concern and flippant scepticism, which mirrors the readers' responses. It is also in the juxtaposing of pop-culture and theology: a theology of the market place, the aeroplane cabin, the rock-star, the filmgoer and the madman.

Rushdie's narrator in *The Ground Beneath Her Feet* is a thinly veiled Rushdie figure, a photographer of the whole mad world (a novelist, get it?) who describes himself in the first chapter in this way:

> Long ago I developed a knack for invisibility. It allowed me to go right up to the actors in the world's drama, the sick, the dying, the crazed, the mourning, the rich, the greedy, the ecstatic, the bereft, the angry, the murderous, the secretive, the bad, the children, the good, the newsworthy; to shimmy into their charmed space, into the midst of their rage or grief or transcendent arousal, to penetrate the defining instant of their being-in-the world and get my fucking picture.[10]

---

9. Salman Rushdie, *The Ground Beneath Her Feet* (London: Jonathan Cape, 1999), 347–8.
10. Rushdie, *The Ground Beneath Her Feet*, 14.

Again we see Rushdie's preoccupation with mirroring, representing, filming the world. Is this an attempt to understand, or to relinquish the possibility of understanding, and merely to report: There it is, I have seen it, I have taken its picture; it is mad, diverse, frightening, exhilarating, but I do not have to be *it.* I merely 'get my fucking picture' and get out. This photographer, narrator, friend and hanger-on of Ormus the visionary, is a god-like figure, invisible, omnipresent, omniscient but unmoved finally. He is also the agent of popular culture, its *necessary agent,* moving in and out of the intimate, charmed spaces of the culture, alive to its archetypes, the zeitgeist of the culture, indiscriminatingly jamming together the visceral and the transcendent in his reports to the hungry world.

Like that other blockbuster novelist of the intelligentsia, JM Coetzee, the utter secularity of Rushdie's project is underscored with a gaping question mark. Beneath JM Coetzee's form of postmodernity, with its Beckett-like silences and reticence,[11] and beneath Rushdie's very different chaotic linguistic exuberances, both writers address a world where social and personal transformations are storming the barricades, from both directions, and incessantly. And gaping questions about meaning-making remain. Do you embrace the figures thrusting themselves perilously into new forms, new social configurations, new types of sacredness, who come clothed in popular motley gear: political activists, ad-men and women, pop-stars, film-makers, actors, novelists. If you do decide to embrace, and even to try on their kind of postmodern, pop-culture outfits, you will be licensing yourself to embrace, and also to read, watch, sift, taste, compare, wonder, enjoy, assent and decline, endlessly. This is not *not* asking the questions, but asking them again and again, in the onrush. In the middle of ordinary life in the capitalist West at the beginning of the twenty-first century.

Aboriginal popular music by bands such as Coloured Stone, the Wurumpi Band, Archie Roach, Yothu Yindi, and by white bands such as Midnight Oil decided over the nineties to tap mainstream popular culture, bringing together some of the most ancient cultural beliefs and forms, with contemporary technology. Both Midnight Oil and Yothu Yindi sang at the 2000 Sydney Olympics to huge global audiences. Yothu Yindi, headed by Mandawuy Yunupingu, and supported by state of the art technology, and white collaborators, sang their by now legendary song 'Treaty'. As most popular music fans know, this song was released twice, the first time in February 1991, and the second time as a dance remix, sung almost

11. See for example Coetzee's Booker winning novel *Disgrace* (London: Secker and Warburg, 1999).

totally in Gumatj language, the tongue of the Yolgnu people. The lyrics of the first version were written in collaboration with white musicians Peter Garrett and Paul Kelly, and the production employed indigenous sounds and instruments almost as special features in the song and video. By contrast, 'Treaty' 2, is sung in Gumatj, with a few rewritten English phrases, and the video depicts Yolgnu people dancing, relaxed, and enjoying themselves. Musicologist Philip Hayward[12] argues that both versions do much to capture and preserve the uniqueness of Yolgnu culture, and they do this through an ongoing dialogue between traditional Yolgnu culture, contemporary, ordinary Yolgnu life, and modern technologies.

This strongly political, culturally subtle popular song, when performed at the Olympic Games, was for many Australians a very moving, even sacred experience, tying together as it did both ancient and contemporary, the law and freedom, and an embodied sense of justice beyond cheap and easy words. How did urban indigenous Australians hear that performance? And Yolgnu? And white Australians of different persuasions? The words of 'Treaty' were in English for the Games, with some Gumatj on the edges:

> Well I heard it on the radio
> And I saw it on the television
> Back in 1988, all those talking politicians
> Words are easy, words are cheap
> Much cheaper than our priceless land
> But promises can disappear
> Just like writing in the sand...
>
> Treaty yeh, Treaty now . . .
>
> The land was never given up
> This land was never bought and sold
> The planting of the Union Jack
> Never changes our law at all

The sounds of stick and didgeridoo interject energetically across the track, and the rhythms of Yolgnu dance movements can be felt in the song, echoed in the video of 'Treaty' 21 especially. The lyrics of the first stanza are laid back, politically acute, using words to hang it on the us-

12. See *Sound Alliances: Indigenous Peoples, Cultural Politics and Popular Music in the Pacific*, edited by Philip Hayward (London: Cassell, 1998).

ers of words used too cheaply. The aboriginal narrator/singer here is an astute popular culture consumer of radio and television, alive to the gaps between representation and reality.[13] The second stanza's lyrics are throw-away utopic, stating with defiance a truth premised beyond the political and historical facts.

As a white urban Australian watching the Olympic opening ceremony on the television, consuming a popular cultural moment, I found it extremely moving, and yes, sacred, in its reverberating, proud, defiant, melodious and postmodern presentation to a global audience. It was moving for me because its cries for social justice for indigenous Australians voiced so powerfully desires I already shared. Its postmodernity was apparent in the wonderful intersections of pre-modern and modern, self-consciously produced with the latest technology for a mass audience, embodying the perhaps impossible call for both a return to origins—the never-changing Yolgnu law, the land never given up—and a modern, politically powerful demand for a Treaty, an agreement between equals. Using dance and music as the vehicle for such sophisticated political demands is also wonderfully political. But it can also be regarded as sacred, an activation of the full self—emotions, beliefs, actions, and good faith—to bring about social justice. Again, the processual and partial realities of history are being recognised. Embodied lives are interacting in history, bringing about change, touched by utopic imagining, but also grounded, rooted in the material—the land, each other, the human ability to recognise and bring about change to unjust social conditions. This is also what I would claim for 'the sacred' here, through the vehicle of popular music and dance, that eroticised, celebratory, human medium, interfacing with sacredness.

But can this broad category of social justice be claimed within the context of the sacred? Justice is so often a category in excess of the status quo, always uncomfortable for the stakeholders of the status quo, coming often from the minority who are oppressed. It also involves a recognition of identity as open to difference, to production by what we've come to call the postmodern condition: hybridity, new agency, new forms of identity to be negotiated, but always with respect to and in tension with history. As Boyarin argues in *A Radical Jew: Paul and the Politics of Identity*,[14] writing of Genesis and its editors about the kind of society they have constructed/

13. See Marcia Langton's, 'Well, I heard it on the radio and I saw it on the Television' (Australian Film Commission, North Sydney 1993). 93ff.

14. Cited in Brett, Mark, *Genesis: Procreation and the Politics of Identity* (London: Routledge, 2000), 146. Brett's whole volume, written for Routledge's Old Testament Read-

envisaged: it is '. . . one that will allow for stubborn hanging on to ethnic, cultural specificity but in a context of deeply felt and enacted human solidarity'. Many religious traditions have a long history of struggle with issues of social justice, sometimes themselves being the perpetrators of injustice, the refusal to accept difference and cultural specificity; sometimes being the strongest agent in crying out for such justice in the name of a god who can and does embrace all differences, beyond human understanding and ability.

So, do we bother to *experience and read* popular culture, in all its diverse manifestations, in order to comprehend the movements of spirit, the possible new configurations of the sacred? Of course, and of course. It will not be a reading of signs in search of The Sign. It will be reading as process, the place and the activity of debate, dissent, laughter, celebration, disgruntlement, dismissal and assent, this kind of reading. In other words, it will involve being immersed in everyday life, its throwaway lines, its local blasphemies, its local honourings, and it will involve a measuring and sifting of all these ephemera, to see where they unfold their wings, where they fly to meet the deepest longings and needs of people. Without such openness, we blot out the everyday lives and quests of most people. As Parkins writes in her essay 'Oprah Winfrey's Change Your life TV', taking off from Durkheim:

> . . . the religious, the sacred, the spiritual, are linked with and located in the world of everyday life; they are a response to everyday life because of its very patterns of repetition and quiddity. Everyday life for many . . . is profoundly imbued with spirituality; popular culture is suffused with it; the most-watched talk show is always talking about it. Cultural studies needs to get over its embarrassment and start talking about it too.[15]

---

ings series, is relevant to this extended discussion concerning sacredness and social justice.

15. Parkins, 142.

Works Cited

Brett, Mark. *Genesis: Procreation And The Politics Of Identity* (London: Routledge, 2000).

Clément, Catherine and Kristeva, Julia. *The Feminine And The Sacred*, translated by Jane Marie Todd (Palgrave: Columbia University Press, 2001).

Hill, Barry. *The Rock: Travelling To Uluru* (Sydney: Allen & Unwin, 1994).

Central Land Council, Pitjantjatjara Council and the Mutitjulu Community, *Sharing the Park: Anangu Initiatives In Ayres Rock Tourism* (Alice Springs: Institute for Aboriginal Development, 1991).

Coetzee, JM. *Disgrace* (London: Secker and Warburg, 1999).

Hayward, Philip. (editor), *Sound Alliances: Indigenous Peoples, Cultural Politics and Popular Music in the Pacific* (London: Cassell, 1998).

Langton, Marcia. 'Well, I Heard It On The Radio And I Saw It On The Television' (North Sydney: Australian Film Commission, 1993).

Marcus, Julie. 'The Journey Out To The Centre: The Cultural Appropriation of Ayers Rock', in *Race Matters: Indigenous Australians and 'Our' Society*, edited by Cowlishaw, Gillian and Morris, Barry (Canberra: Aboriginal Studies Press, 1997), 29–51.

Morris, Meaghan. 'Banality In Culutral Studies', in *Logics of Television: Essays In Culutral Criticism*, edited by by Patricia Mellanchamp (Bloomington, Indiana University Press), 14–4.

Parkins, Wendy and Brabazon, Tara, editors. *Continuum: Journal of Media and Cultural Studies*, 15/2 (July 2001): 141–144.

Rushdie, Salman. *The Ground Beneath Her Feet* (London: Jonathan Cape, 1999).

Tacey, David. *Edge of the Sacred: Transformation In Australia* (North Blackburn: HarperCollins, 1995).

TISM, 'De Rigeurmortis' (song) (Mushroom Records, Australia, 2001).

Chapter Two

Postmodern Rituals: Contemporary Australia Responds to Bali

After Bali, a range of public rituals took place in Australia to remember those who had been killed in the bombing. In Melbourne, the most visible and collective ritual was the laying of flowers by members of the public on the steps of the State Parliament building, at the highly visible apex of Bourke Street in Melbourne. This was a much-publicised event which took place over a period of two weeks. It was a riveting and moving sight/site for many people, who left notes expressing grief and regret, promises of remembrance, and of revenge. The choice of the site, and what would happen there, was prompted by talk-back listeners to Melbourne Radio 3AW's Neil Mitchell, who called in with many different suggestions as to where and why the laying of flowers should take place. This essay seeks to understand the processes and purposes of the popular, public rituals after Bali, asking who made them, what was made, and how popular—that is, open to formation by those not primarily and *directly* connected with the mass media and party politics—were the constructions? Further, in calling such an event a 'postmodern ritual', the essay will inaugurate an analysis, through cultural studies methodologies, of the attributes of public rituals in contemporary Western cultures.

The history of anthropological studies of ritual is the study of earlier *religious* explanations that became increasingly complicated by concepts of *ideology*. It is also the history of *structuralist* thought moving towards *poststructuralism*. Anthropology's early claims to be the disciplinary site of ritual studies were most often articulated through studies of religion.[1] The long evolution in anthropological approaches to ritual develops from

1. For an excellent overview of the disciplinary imbrications of anthropology, studies of religion and ritual, see John K Nelson, *The Anthropology of Religion: A Field Statement for the Department of Anthropology* (Berkeley: University of California, 1990).

the work of Emile Durkheim, *The Elementary Forms of the Religious Life*,[2] in which the sacred/profane dichotomy stood as the overarching concept; through to mid-century anthropological questioning of this dichotomy,[3] and more recent expansions and responses to Durkheim's work;[4] to the important genealogical work of Victor Turner who placed increasing stress on the openness of participants expectations in the performance of rituals; to the stress on *ideology* in social ritual, enabled by the 1970s work of Geertz and Foucault.

Moving beyond purely religious explanations of ritual, the influential anthropology of Clifford Geertz offered broader definitions of *ideology* in relation to ritual. In the essay 'Ideology as a Cultural System', Geertz saw ideology as 'a response to strain'[5] in society, a 'confluence of socio-psychological strain and an absence of cultural resources by means of which to make sense of the strain, each exacerbating the other'.[6] In his description of the workings of ideologies he comes close to setting the stage for contemporary public rituals and their necessity, when he writes: 'Whatever ideologies may be—projections of unacknowledged fears, disguises for ulterior motives, phatic expressions of group solidarity—they are, most distinctively, maps of problematic social reality and matrices for the creation of collective conscience'.[7]

Anthropologist Michael Taussig, informed by poststructural approaches in the 1980s and 1990s, expands understandings of ritual into the postmodern, connecting religious and ideological with individual, experiential, embodied accounts of ritual. While still working within the study of religion in society, Taussig has necessarily and fruitfully compli-

2. Emile Durkheim, *The Elementary Forms of the Religious Life*, translated by Joseph Swain (London: Allen and Unwin, 1963).
3. See for example the excellent article on distinctions between religion, ritual and ceremony by Jack R Goody, 'Religion and Ritual: The Definitional Problem', in *British Journal of Sociology* 12 (1961): 142–163.
4. See for example David Ketzer, *Ritual, Politics, and Power* (New Have: Yale University Press, 1988).
5. Clifford Geertz, *The Interpretations of Culture: Selected Essays* (New York: Basic Books, 1973), 219.
6. Geertz, *The Interpretations of Culture* 220.
7. Geertz, *The Interpretations of Culture*. For Marxist critiques of Geertz's concepts of ideology and ritual, see Talal Asad, 'Anthropology and the Analysis of Ideology', in *Man* 14, (1979): 607–627, and 'Anthropological Conceptions of Religion: Reflections on Geertz', in *Man* 18, 237–259; and Bob Scholte, 'The Charmed Circle of Geertz's Hermeneutics: A Neo-Marxist Critique', in *Critique of Anthropology* 6/1: 5–15.

cated the study of ritual in the light of secularisation and globalisation, as well as at the micro level of lived experiences.

Writing within a more immediately and viscerally politicised postmodern context, American sociologist Mark Jurgensmeyer, in his 2002 volume, *Terror in the Mind of God: The Global Rise of Religious Violence*,[8] describes the responses to the September 11, 2001 terrorism of New Yorkers, who set up, around lampposts, or along vacant block fences, little temporary neighbourhood shrines, leaving flowers, messages and candles, as well as photocopied messages—'Have you seen this man/woman . . . please contact' posters. Jurgensmeyer was moved by what he describes as these temporary shrines, experiencing them as fitting, popular, spontaneous expressions of sentiment: that is, of grief and the desire to remember. When questioned at the 2002 *Religion and the Arts* conference if such 'moving' 'temporary shrines' could also be read as *sentimental*, and as places around which signs of hatred, patriotism, rallying cries for American vengeance also circled, Jurgensmeyer demurred, replying that grieving citizens also had a need to express anger. The strands of religious/ritual and ideological response entwined here need some investigation.

As noted above, by the 1970s Geertz's work has begun to move away from the purely religious explanations of ritual, drawing out the interconnectedness between public ritual/ceremony, and the workings and pressures of ideology within a society. In his description of the ways in which rituals work, both in traditional and to a certain extent modern societies, he compounds the ideological aspects of ritual: 'In a ritual, the world as lived and the world as imagined, fused under the agency of a single set of symbolic forms, turns out to be the same world.'[9] This is still a basically purist and religious description of ritual, but it is already beginning to embrace elements beyond 'the religious', paving the way for the uneasy—postmodern, mongrel—fusions, or impossible desires for such fusion, evident in contemporary postmodern rituals. How helpful is a concept of 'postmodern, mongrel ritual' in considering such different public demonstrations of grief, anger, revenge, forgiveness and bewilderment as the death of Princess Diana, the road side memorials along the edges of freeways, and the Bali memorial services? How fleeting, temporal and quickly past can such a demonstration be, and still be considered a ritual in any significant way?

8. Mark Jurgensmeyer, *Terror in the Mind of God: The Global Rise of Religious Violence* (Berkeley: University of California Press, 2002).
9. Geertz, *The Interpretations of Culture*, 112.

In reading the 'temporary shrine' at Parliament House in Melbourne, I came across a number of highly personalised messages amongst the sea of flowers, but two cards stand out: one read 'Christ will win in the end' and the other, with a slightly more poetic touch, said 'The Rosary will strangle al Qaeda'. Neil Mitchell commented that such a memorial expressed the powerlessness and futility of people in the face of terror. With such a range of responses, how do we read the purposes of this 'ritual'? How do we begin to think about the connections between ritual and ideology in post-modern societies? In what ways was this a ritual, if at all?

In order to address these questions—to give them historical framework—I found it helpful to consider the work on Aboriginal ritual of contemporary cultural studies academic Stephen Muecke. Informed by the work of Michael Taussig, José Gil, and Michel de Certeau, Muecke has recently written about the importance of what he calls Aboriginal practices or rituals—what he sees as the meeting of philosophy and magic. He values in these rituals the 'immediate' and 'performative', the 'transformative' and 'relational', drawing together as these rituals do the individual body, the communal body and the country. In this context, Muecke critiques Western academic procedures, which, he argues, only falteringly grasp the experiential and processual (my word) nature of the forces alive in Aboriginal rituals. Muecke argues that the workings of Aboriginal culture are obfuscated by the Western drive towards 'representationalism'—the incessant *reading* of texts (rituals, philosophies, symbols, myths, narratives). He claims of Aboriginal ritual, that 'it is *movement* going on here, not meaning; rapidity, not *logos*'.[10] (I will return to this concept of movement and the refusal of fixed meaning, which is, I think, valuable in considering contemporary popular rituals).

For example, of the work of early anthropologist WEH Stanner, which he both honours and critiques, Muecke writes:

> He is floundering around with a circular representationalist model where 'things' have to be objectified and made metaphysical, converted to images, and fed back into the ritual complex from which they originally emerged. The process he is describing is not an Aboriginal process of understanding, but the process of his own science's rationalizations of 'Aboriginal religion'.[11]

10. Stephen Muecke, 'Travelling the Subterranean River of Blood: Philosophy and Magic in Cultural Studies', in *Cultural Studies* 13/1 (1999): 9.
11. Muecke, 'Travelling', 9.

With his comparative emphasis on the processual and performative nature of Aboriginal cultural production, Muecke is seeking to provide non-indigenous readers with a critique of their own academic, scientistic, representationalist approaches which, he claims, are missing the 'immediate relations between objects, things, feelings, words, and music'.[12] Muecke is aligned here with the anthropology of Michael Taussig, which he reads as critiquing 'anthropology's reduction to the symbolic, the function being to create understandable and exploitable "traditions" out of the force and magic of the primitive'.[13] For Muecke, performance and ontology come together in what is arguably an idealist discourse. Muecke is not explicitly critiquing Western *rituals*, but rather the academic modes of recording such rituals. However, my argument hinges around the *implicit comparison* between such (idealising) representations of Aboriginal ritual and what might be called hybrid, mongrel, postmodern rituals.[14] I am in the complicted position here of both disclaiming the idealising implications of Muecke's work, but of wanting to incorporate the notion of movement, immediacy and performativity into the discussion of a range of postmodern rituals. The phenomena to which I am here attempting to apply such qualities or affects are of course very different to the Aboriginal contexts as described by Muecke, and are themselves temporal, moving, and self-reflexively performative.

Contemporary rituals demonstrably share many worrying, persistent ideological features (colonialist, xenophobic and reductionist: recall 'The

12. Muecke, 'Travelling', 10.
13. Muecke, 'Travelling', 10.
14. The term 'postmodern ritual' seems appropriate here in the light of developments in Anthropology, and in Western societies, across the twentieth century. Anthropology, which has dwelled so much on non-Western and religious/sacred communities for its objects of study, has been coming to grips, along with Sociology, with the accelerating effects of secularisation in the West, and with what has been argued, in postmodern debates, to be the return of the repressed sacred in the West. See Mary Douglas' work for a systematic description of the effects of modernity on religion; and Peter Berger who discusses the crisis of religion in the West and the crisis in secularity's 'myth of progress'. See for example Peter Berger, *Facing Up to Modernity: Excursions in Society, Politics and Religion* (New York: Basic Books, 1977); *Religion and America: Spiritual Life in a Secular Age*, edited by Mary Douglas and Steven Tipton (Boston: Beacon Press, 1983). For more contemporary readings on this conjunction between postmodernity and the sacred, see for example the University of Chicago Press series, *Religion and Postmodernism*, edited by Mark C Taylor; John D Caputo and Michael J Scanlon, *God, the Gift, and Postmodernism* (Bloomington and Indianapolis: Indiana University Press, 1999); Catherine Clément and Julia Kristeva, *The Feminine and the Sacred* (New York: Columbia University Press, 2001).

Rosary will strangle al Qaeda'). But other more processual, tentative, ad hoc, often gauche, and valuable features are at the same time traceable in these *popular* ceremonies. Further, I would want to argue, contra Muecke, that *reading* the features of postmodern rituals, seeking meaning, analysing the forces at work, trying to decipher the ambivalence of such events, helpfully complicates what Muecke critiques as the Western mindset's representationalist practices. Such *reading* is what contemporary participants are doing constantly, even *as they participate*, to varying degrees.

In contrast to the purer images of Aboriginal ritual given to us by Muecke (ritual seen as repeated, as more sustaining, as more attached to the land, to specific relations with and sites in the land), the arena of contemporary ritual-making is formed by a hybrid, one might say *mongrel*, range of phenomena, made of diverse sets of conventions and symbols, and with multiple possible affects and effects. How does one measure, or think about contemporary Australian rituals, those emanating often simultaneously from the state, from the media, from churches, temples and mosques, as well as from individuals—dare one say from popular culture?—in the comparative light of the supposedly true rituals (my term) described by Muecke as 'life-affirming', foundational, as 'people arrang(ing) things so that their beliefs about life and death become the effective means of their power'.[15]

In the Domain in Sydney on the Sunday after the massacre in Bali[16] a hybrid event of memorialisation. took place. It sought to hear the voices of a range of Australians (in what could be read as a '*PC*' multicultural way); it was shaped by mass-media participation: the iconic, ubiquitous Geraldine Doogue MC-ing, the live-crosses to Bali, as well as around Australia, to pick up the Prime Minister etc; it presented various religious traditions in a loose-boned way, with Christian and Hindu elements, with Lakemba Islamic college students taking part in the flower ceremony, a didge player accompanying. We are here in the territory of 'popular culture', *and* of institutional culture—media, state, religion. This event could be read simply in terms of hegemonic and institutional manipulating towards potentially nationalist ends of 'the popular'. However, it is possible to see these modern rituals as occupying a problematic and postmodern, hybrid third space, one in which all these elements are detectable and interpenetrating. What do we make of such a third space?

15. Muecke, 'Travelling', 15.
16. Australian Bali Memorial Day ceremony, ABC television broadcast, Sunday October 20, 2002.

Corrie Perkins, writing in *The Sunday Age*, used a range of sources regarding the events in Bali and the rituals being performed in their aftermath. She quotes Anglican Archbishop Peter Watson describing such gatherings: 'It is really important for us all to admit something really terrible has happened, to let our feelings come out . . . These moments, and these kinds of gatherings allow (such expressions).' Rabbi Ralph Genende is quoted: 'We need ceremony, we need an outlet for the enormous amount of feeling that has been unleashed by this event . . . When you share grief you diminish something of the acuteness of it.' The Rabbi is also quoted, perhaps contradictorily, saying: 'One of the things we can do as a country is to stand together and confront this kind of evil.' Tim Costello, a Baptist spokesperson, said there needed to be rallying points: '. . . a park or a hall or municipal gardens' for those unconnected to churches. 'There has to be a place where people can come and light a candle, hear a piece of music, or hear the names of the victims read . . . It has been a national tragedy and we are all in this together.' Never lost for evangelical words, Costello goes on to reflect on the nature of Christian culture:

> The one thing about churches in a more Christian culture—you actually have a strong sense of where to go. The symbols remain alive in your memory—the cross, the candles, the hymns. But for many, that sense of being together is not all that clear. Where do people go? Their confusion is very apparent now, and I suspect many people on Sunday will take the initiatives themselves.[17]

Perhaps such a tragic time should provoke even the most garrulous or 'representationalist' academic observers to suspend analysis and simply to participate? After all, do not these public acts overtly call for a forgetting—or at least suspending—of individual, critical self, the other who stands aside and observes, and for an invoking of the participatory self who seeks through ritual to join emotionally in the experiences of the other's grief/anger. In other words, what use cultural semiotics?

In an early 1990's debate about the nature of popular culture as practice, John Frow critiques what he sees as Michel de Certeau's ethnography of actions, his stress on the 'singularity and particularity of practices', arguing that both 'uses and doings are codified (that is, They are texts) . . . (and that) the appeal to a pristine (and invisible) *experience* of the text is

17. Corrie Perkins, 'A Day to Share the Pain and Start the Healing', in *The Sunday Age*, 20 October 2002, 2.

both unwarranted and in principle dangerous.'[18] In an essay in response to Frow, Tony Schirato argues that

> Frow . . . would either have practice deliver up itself, unmediated, or, and this amounts to much the same thing, he would have it delivered up through a pure and objective scientific gaze and discourse. Frow is aware that the notion of practice exposes the claims of science, but the desire to know and explain makes him forget what he already knows.[19]

The thorny tension between practice and reading, experience and analysis, is succinctly expressed here. It is this same split that concerned Muecke. But a middle ground opens up in Schirato's discussion, a third space where the necessary discriminating and reflection, even of a rudimentary kind, occurs, in order to decide how one will or will not participate. This tension typifies contemporary public Western ritual, I am arguing, and can in fact be thought of as its highly *valuable* characteristic. It is the self-reflexive, ambivalent and one might even add reticent, suspicious way in which many participants enter into such postmodern rituals which places them in a different category to traditional rituals.

In the case of the Bali rituals, this ambivalence is made up of great individual and communal pain, and the need for support, amongst many participants, together with an 'Australian' wariness about institutionality—religion, media, politics—and other orchestrated elements. Most Western participants in such postmodern, public rituals are not practised in what are experienced by many as institutionally constructed, 'fixed' religious symbol and ritual. This essay is arguing that it is the reticence and ambivalence of the Bali ritual events—the demonstrated compulsion to express almost inexpressible sorrow and sympathy felt by so many, together with bewilderment, anger, and even national outrage, which is the defining and valuable trait of these transient, mongrel, postmodern rituals. In this reticence there can be seen both the need to read, understand, analyse, and the desire and willingness to participate before any reading or understanding can take place, if at all. Doubt and participation are not, of course, mutually exclusive.

---

18. John Frow, 'Michel de Certeau and the Practice of Representation', in *Cultural Studies* 5, (1991): 59.
19. Tony Schirato, 'My Space or Yours? De Certeau, Frow and the Meanings of Popular Culture', in *Cultural Studies* 7 (1993): 282.

Michel de Certeau describes the space of a postmodern tension, the ghostlike terrain of popular practice, where what he calls consumers (those 'unrecognised producers, poets of their own acts, silent discoverers of their own paths in the jungle of functionalist rationality'[20] enact both participation and discrimination:

> In the technocratically constructed, written, and functionalized space in which the consumers move about, their trajectories form unforeseeable sentences, partly unseeable paths across a space. Although they are composed with the vocabularies of established languages (those of television, newspapers, supermarkets, or museum sequences) . . . the trajectories trace out the ruses of other interests and desires that are neither determined nor captured by the systems in which they develop.[21]

If we accept de Certeau's hopeful notion of consumers and their agency—'the ruses of other interests and desires',—there is the potential to see cultural usefulness in these mongrel cultural events. I would like to be able to agree with his optmistic notion of cultural production, as subversive, contextualised, heterogeneous bricolage, and even with his optimism that the effects of such production are 'without capitalizing . . . without taking control over time'.[22] However, there are grounds for reservation about such optimisim in the light of the much more *ideologically mongrel* nature of such practices observed 'after Bali'; in some of those microscopic, but '*less cohesive*' effects produced in the interstices of the popular outpourings of emotion: 'Christ will win in the end'. 'The rosary will strangle al Qaeda'. Fundamentalism breeding fundamentalism? Apocalyptic time invoked to produce a 'taking control over time'—not, I think, what de Certeau was imagining, and not of course a product of 'popular culture' alone, but shared with many state, media and religious institutions.

For me there remains, however, a usable and helpful metaphor for such ambivalence in de Certeau's celebrating the *refusal to take control over time*, of experiencing the weight and the loss of time, its *more than human* architecture. This response is markedly different to, and subversive of, the political response of taking up arms, issuing edicts, talk of pre-emptive

20. Michel de Certeau, *The Practice of Everyday Life*, translated by Steven Rendell (London: University of California Press, 1984), xviii.
21. de Certeau, *The Practice of Everyday Life*, xviii.
22. de Certeau, *The Practice of Everyday Life*, xx.

strikes, taking control, all with their own fundamentalist metaphors of good and evil.

What is the role and the potential of mongrel, contemporary ritual? Although little neighbourhood shrines might also be rallying points of aggression, it has been the argument of this essay that it is the simultaneous willingness of many citizens to participate, *together with* the ambivalence, questioning and scepticism of the effects of such participation, and even the necessary acknowledgement of violent responses within that mix, which define contemporary rituals *per se*. Such a multiple response—participation with ambivalence—seems far from Muecke's idealising of Aboriginal ritual. However, it shares with Muecke's understanding of indigenous ritual a desire to embrace ritual as a moving out beyond logos, or fixed, credal meaning. The rituals of contemporary Australia are of course structured by this current historical moment, and more broadly by the vertiginous conditions of contemporary Western subjects in the context of terrorism. The argument of this essay is that such postmodern rituals simultaneously evidence a suspicious, ambivalence *and* desire for participation. This is far from a simple demand for 'The Logos', but it is still an understandable acknowledgement of desire for meaning.

Works Cited

De Certeau, Michel. *The Practice of Everyday Life,* Translated by *Steven Rendell* (London: University of California Press, 1984).

Durkheim, Emile. *Elementary Forms of the Religious Life,* translated by Joseph Swain (London: Allen and Unwin, 1963).

Foucault, Michel. *Power/Knowledge: Selected Interviews and Other Writings 1972°1977* (New York: Pantheon Books, 1981).

Frow, John. 'Michel de Certeau and the Practice of Representation', in *Cultural Studies* 5 (1991): 52–60.

Geertz, Clifford. *The Interpretations of Culture: Selected Essays* (New York: Basic Books, 1973).

Jurgensmeyer, Mark. *Terror in the Mind of God: The Global Rise of Religious Violence* (Berkeley: University of California Press, 2002).

Muecke, Stephen. 'Travelling the Subterranean River of Blood: Philosophy and Magic in Cultural Studies', in *Cultural Studies* 13/1 (1999): 1–17.

Perkins, Corrie. 'A Day to Share the Pain and Start the Healing', in *The Sunday Age*, October 20, 2002, 2.

Schirato, Tony. 'My Space or Yours? De Certeau, Frow and the Meanings of Popular Culture', in *Cultural Studies* 7 (1993): 282–91.

Taussig, Michael. *Shamanism, Colonialism, and the Wild Man: A Study in Terror and Healing* (Chicago: Chicago University Press, 1987).

----*Mimesis and Alterity: A Particular History of the Senses* (New York and London: Routledge, 1993).

Turner, Victor. *The Ritual Process: Structure and Anti-Structure* (Chicago: Aldine Press, 1969).

Chapter Three

The Impossible Infinite: Les Murray, Poetry, and the Sacred

In 1983 provocative and idiosyncratic Australian poet Les Murray published a volume entitled '*The People's Otherworld*'. At the heart of that middle volume of Murray's work is a poem about grace. Its title is 'Equanimity,' which the poem sees as a place 'where the farmer has done enough struggling-to-survive / for one day, and the artist rests from theory--/ where all are, in short, off the high comparative horse / of their identity'.[1] It is a place, or time, we are told, 'beneath effort', where 'lifelong plenishment' is found or given. This is a landscape of deepest humanness, we are told, a place from which 'all holiness speaks'. This equanimity is represented in multiple ways: it is the 'on-off grace' that attends the movement of birds; it is light which 'makes some smile, some grimace'; it is the place from which Christ 'spoke to people most often'; it is a painting of equality, and a landscape of 'infinite detailed extent / like God's attention'. But strangely, in order to represent such fullness the poem centres around two absences: the first is a 'sometimes glimpsed' light or grace, and the second is Murray's old, familiar, rancorous railing against human failure to glimpse such grace:

> there is only love; there are no Arcadias.
> Whatever its variants of meat-cuisine, worship, divorce,
> human order has at heart
> an equanimity. Quite different from inertia, it's a place
> where the churchman's not defensive, the indignant aren't on the *qui vive*,
> the loser has lost interest, the accountant is truant to remorse,
> where the farmer has done enough struggling-to-survive
> for one day, and the artist rests from theory –

1. Les Murray, *Collected Poems* (North Ryde: Angus & Robertson, 1991), 159.

where all are, in short, off the high comparative horse
of their identity.
Almost beneath notice, as attainable as gravity, it is
a continuous recovering moment. Pity the high madness
that misses it continually, ranging without rest between
assertion and unconsciousness,
the sort that makes hell seem a height of evolution.
Through the peace beneath effort
(even within effort: quiet air between the bars of our attention)
comes unpurchased lifelong plenishment;
Christ spoke to people most often on this level
especially when they chattered about kingship and the Romans;
all holiness speaks from it.[2]

This, strangely, is the middle stanza of a poem about peace, grace and equanimity. The poem needs, it seems, to establish the possibility of such fullness on the back of old enemies, to invoke ancient wounds and faults in order to clear the ground for holiness. There is an inherent tension, if not outright contradiction here—one that this essay will probe, not from any 'high comparative horse,' but in order to ask the following questions: How does the poetry of Les Murray seek to represent the sacred? And is language capable of representing the sacred?

If we look again at this poem extolling 'the peace beneath effort / (even within effort . . .)' we can see the tensions writ large: how to speak of God, the absolute other, without taking on the God-mantle; how to receive 'unpurchased life-long plenishment' while 'purchasing' it in the very act and effort of representation. In his essay 'Les Murray and Poetry's Otherworld', American critic Paul Kane generously describes such tensions as part of 'a dialectic, if not a dialogue' with Murray's readers. Kane's essay is on the edge of critique of Murray's poetics, but most often lapses back, I would argue, into a warm praise of his themes and modes of poetry that grapple with the sacred. Following Kane for a moment, we might describe Murray's three central poetic modes or impulses as: firstly, use of a 'middle style and a sacramental (or ritual) temperament,' with a democratic sense of ordinary life as the locus of the sacred; secondly, a sense of human, cultural convergence, or as Murray himself puts it, 'an enactment of a longed-for fusion of all three cultures [Aboriginal, country and city], a fusion which, as yet perhaps, can only exist in art, or in blessed moments when

2 Murray, *Collected Poems*, 159.

power and ideology are absent';[3] and thirdly, a propheticism, in the forms of both social critic or satirist, and as a messenger of the divine. This latter often involves 'silence' and a proclaimed attendance of 'something beyond imagining', an understanding of the artist as 'one who makes things the value of which is located beyond death'.[4]

So, for Kane, Murray's poetic representations of the sacred employ a ritual and democratic vernacular, a sense of cultural fusion of ideologically disparate tribes, and propheticism. There is certainly 'effort' and dare I say 'theory' behind all of these supposedly post-ideological impulses, but perhaps it is the kind of effort that allows for that 'quiet air between the bars of our attention', that possibility of grace. As a critic I am in awe of Murray's artistic desire to represent the something beyond representation, but it is both an admiring and a skeptical awe. And in reading Murray, I find the skepticism must have equal play with the admiration. Simply to be directed against effort or theory is tantamount to being told by the artist: 'trust me.' My democratic response to this directive would be: 'trust and test.'

So this essay will give equal time to skepticism and admiration, and offer a number of readings that seek the limits of both trust and analysis. First, it is helpful to consider the contexts into which Murray's poetry arrives, for this individual reader, and more broadly in relation to contemporary theological debates. In doing this, it is necessary first to acknowledge that the context of 'Australian secularism,' to use a gross shorthand for the moment, and its readings of Murray, can hardly be touched in this essay. One of the most humorous, colloquially irreverent and resistant among these responses is Ken Bolton's poem *Untimely Meditations*:

In the mid 70s
I became aware
of an irritating irregular din,
becoming quite insistent
-- things beginning with 'I'
appropriately.
It was Les Murray
Les told us

3. Les Murray, *Persistence in Folly: Selected Prose Writings* (Sydney: Angus & Robertson, 1984), 24.
4. Les Murray cited in Paul Kane, 'Les Murray and Poetry's Otherworld', in *Australian Poetry, Romanticism and Negativity* (Cambridge: Cambridge University Press, 1996), 200.

'Where's
the beef?'
as if poems were a sandwich
and his
had dinkum verities
and content, while ours were that relativistic nonsense
you learn at unis,
not very sustaining.
This was 'the City and the Country' theme.[5]

Bolton's is an altogether other, secular response to 'Les' that can find no redeeming features in the preacherly, insistent presentation of 'dinkum verities / and content'. Its humour is informed and seems to come from a deep, alienated place that has no room for Murray's poetics. However, the context I want to create in this essay is one that seeks both to question and illuminate Murray's poetics of the sacred. This context can be introduced through two brief descriptions of what might be called 'postmodern' and 'post-colonial' theologies: the first is from an essay entitled 'Infinity, Insomnia and the (im)possibility of theology', in which Australian theologian Stephen Curkpatrick explicates the work of Emmanuel Levinas. He does so within a poststructural, Derridean framework that sees that for any writing that approaches the divine, 'Witness to the infinite is betrayed when it is translated into a theme ("the said"). This "said" as the predicting grammar of the word "God", must constantly be unsaid in order to bear witness to the infinite'.[6]

To gloss this idea, Curkpatrick quotes Levinas arguing that 'language is already skepticism, haunting rational thought, contesting the solidification of thought in the "said"'.[7] And the second description of a current theological context is from Jamie S Scott, a Canadian post-colonial and religious studies critic, from his 1998 essay 'Geographies of the Sacred and Postcolonial Literatures'. He emphasises

> the precariousness of our own sacred contexts, the historical accident of our own sacred locations . . . in a heightened awareness

5. Ken Bolton, *Untimely Meditations and other poems* (Adelaide: Wakefield Press, 1997), 37.
6. Stephen Curkpatrick, 'Infinity, Insomnia and the (im)possibility of Theology', in *Pacifica* 17/1 (2004): 28.
7. Emmanuel Levinas, *Otherness than Being; or, Beyond Essence*, translated by Alphonso Lingis (Boston: Hague, 1991), 44.

> of the relativity of all locatedness, human or divine. Post-colonial writings thus offer concrete opportunities for us to discover in ourselves and in our neighbours that simultaneous presence of the seen and the unseen, of the material and the mysterious . . . which animates [a] sense of the sacred.[8]

The negative and the positive-leaning directions of postmodern theology are registered here. Curkpatrick's Levinasian theology constantly questions itself 'so that every "said" is to be constantly "unsaid" in order to bear witness to the infinite, without certifying that the word "God" can serve as an adequate alibi for infinity'.[9] Scott, in contrast, seems more positive as he describes the 'simultaneous presence of the seen and the unseen'.[10] It is true that like Murray Scott has a strong sense of literature—and specifically post-colonial literature—and its ability to represent the sacred. But Scott also has a strong emphasis on the precariousness of such representation. He wants, at an 'ethical level' to 'expose the pretensions to place involved in our narratives, [to . . .] question our proprietory postures, and counter claims to possession [. . .]'.[11] Here he is speaking simultaneously of theological and post-colonial imperatives, of 'critical practices of dislodgement, without which [. . .] narratives become fortified places, abiding cities'.[12]

This essay proposes that Murray's poetics is deeply and dramatically at work within such 'precarious' and 'unsaying' dramas of sacredness. Further, the axiomatic, and at worst, the judgmental and dogmatic certainties and will to authority, of Murray's work undermines a richer impulse, a more self-questioning, less knowing response to the sacred. This second impulse lets fall the pretension to absolutes, those often infuriating Murrayesque axioms, pronouncements, desiderata, binaries, high-horses, and allows the language to reveal its own imperfect, vulnerable, flawed and unabiding capacities. I use 'the language' as the subject of this sentence, not precluding the constructive participation of the author, but allowing in, hopefully, all the healthy skepticism of language to undo itself, and of the reader too, who in the end must discern for herself how to measure Murray's languaged sacred.

---

8. Michael Griffith and James Tulip, editors, *Spirit of Place: Source of the Sacred?* (Sydney: Berget, 1998), 70.
9. Curkpatrick, 'Infinity', 32.
10. Griffith and Tulip, *Spirit of Place*, 70.
11. Scott, in Griffith and Tulip 61.
12. Wesley A Kort, cited in Scott, in Griffith and Tulip, *Spirit of Place*, 61.

A central Murray poem in this context is 'Poetry and Religion', from the 1987 volume *The Daylight Moon*:

> Religions are poems. They concert
> our daylight and dreaming minds, our
> emotions, instinct, breath and native gesture
>
> into the only whole thinking: poetry.
> Nothing's said till it's dreamed out in words
> and nothing's true that figures in words only.
>
> A poem, compared with an arrayed religion,
> may be like a soldier's one short marriage night
> to die and live by. But that is a small religion.
>
> Full religion is the large poem in loving repetition;
> like any poem, it must be inexhaustible and complete
> with turns where we ask Now why did the poet do that?
>
> You can't pray a lie, said Huckleberry Finn;
> you can't poe one either. It is the same mirror:
> mobile, glancing, we call it poetry,
>
> fixed centrally, we call it a religion,
> and God is the poetry caught in any religion,
> caught, not imprisoned. Caught as in a mirror
>
> that he attracted, being in the world as poetry
> is in the poem, a law against closure.
> There'll always be religion around while there is poetry,
>
> or a lack of it. Both are given, and intermittent
> as the action of those birds—crested pigeon, rosella parrot—
> who fly with wings shut, then beating, and again shut.[13]

We are made, technically, to hover over that line break—'inexhaustible and complete / with turns'—to experience the poet's joke about poems as potentially complete, but also 'complete with turns'. My response though is not only to ask the obedient reader's question, 'Now why did the poet do that?' (a question supplied, after all, by the poet) but to wonder at how

13. Murray, *Collected Poems*, 235–36.

language can do things, beyond the poet's control, in this poem. Without second guessing what the poet meant to do, or did accidentally (felicitously or otherwise) it seems that the major drama of the poem is two-fold: a measuring of Murray's playful, serious, languaged claims, and a measuring of how language spins beyond any control of author or reader—wilful, provocative, full of images and the limits of imagery, full of breathtaking assertions and the silliness of such assertions.

Underneath the fruitful central analogy of poetry as religion, religion as poetry—an analogy which flirts with but generally manages to stave off polarisation of thought, a simplistic contrast or difference between poetry and religion—runs a vein of oppositions which the poem both establishes but also seeks to deny or obliterate: daylight and dreaming mind, made singular; emotions concerted playfully, smoothly across the stanza break into 'the only whole thinking'; words as necessary dream tools but also as needing to be put in their place, only a part of the truth; the poem as truth, a place of adoration (loving repetition, analogous to the operations of religion), but also never the same, not reiterable, having a 'law against its closure', being free ('caught, not imprisoned'). The poem's fixed triplet structure gives a regularity; and the sprawling, irregular lines burst open any regularity, allowing in the desired vernacular. The triplet form works through axioms and pronouncements—it can not help itself—even as the poem seeks to break down such certainty: note the playful (or irritating, depending on where you're standing) insistence of 'religions are poems,' 'they concert', 'the only whole thinking: poetry', 'Nothing's said till . . .', 'It is the same mirror . . . ' 'There'll always be religion', etc. It is play, and perhaps all the more provocative for that: alluring and replenishing if you happen to read with the poem's axioms; irritatingly pompous and self-preening—'why did the poet do that?'—and self-sealed if you do not.

But it is the unreadability of two central images that moves beyond this vein of polarities and sets up that second, less conscious, drama of the poem: a measuring of how language spins beyond the control of even these specious polarities. In the image of God caught in a mirror, 'that he attracted;, we are offered a representation of God as poetry, God as the poetry in any religion, God being in the world 'as poetry is in the poem', 'a law against its closure'. How is the everyday reader, seeking the poetry of any poem, expected to look over God's shoulder—to follow the metaphor—into such a mirror? God has attracted the poem and is somehow caught in there, and we humble humans, poets and readers, are promised a vision of God looking out from within. We mustn't force our vision, as poetry is 'given and intermittent'. This brings us back to the tension between effort and the beyond of effort. Is this a tension, or a contradiction here? How are we to read the seductively beautiful final image of 'those birds'—'crested pigeon, rosella parrot—/ who fly with wings shut, then beating, and again shut'? As one of alternating effort and gliding? Or are we being offered the ultimate snake oil here? Trust me, let go, glide, wait for and accept the gift? Does this all equate finally with a choice to trust in the authority of the poet who has been 'given' the poem, and is merely a servant of the divine Giver, but with his own reasons for his turns of language; the poet as authenticate before the truth-bearing of language ('you can't pray a lie')?

The use of the objective correlative of the birds, seen also in 'Equanimity', sets up a further question about human agency and its role in representing the sacred. What is being claimed is that both waiting, givenness, and effort are necessary—wings shut, wings beating—a double claim that seems humble and attentive enough, and not necessarily contradictory. But what room is left for that 'skepticism of language' that Levinas posits? As a reader it is linguistically possible to hear the 'concert' of the poem's first line as 'disconcert'. There is an oddness in the confusion of noun and verb. And further, the less indicated verb here, to concert, or to push or strain or force, undermines the simple lyrical felicity of the former concert. What we have in this poem, it might be argued, is the activity of language—playful, seemingly effortless, not forcing the point, but suggestive, reflective; and simultaneously we have language as axiom, sermon, as binaristic, scheming to establish or claim truth, saying even as it pretends simply to suggest. Abrahm's mirror and lamp metaphor is relevant here: do we have in Murray's poem a structure claiming merely to be a mirror—'mobile, glancing'—but necessarily repressing its own stage-lighting, its effort-ful design upon us?

What is the effect of the poem in terms of contemporary theological contexts? Does language here ask us to trust it, and then betray us, in equal parts? If so, how then are we as critical and discerning readers to approach this doubleness? One instinctive response is to catch Murray in his own spotlight, put him up against the wall, make him admit his culpability in the whole thing. After all, if he's claiming that the poet is the one who seeds all those 'turns' in the poem, isn't he to be held accountable for letting us down—allowing us to see the stitching and the flaws? But another, perhaps more generous response is to acknowledge here the overwhelming workings of language—always unsaying (doubting, failing to accomplish, constantly aware of the other possibilities it excludes). This unsaying may be philosophical and overt, as it is for Levinas or Derrida, or it may be enacted both consciously and unconsciously, in the language of the poets. In this context I want to co-opt Murray's vision of effort, and the beyond of effort, of gift and waiting, with the work of representation, in a slightly aslant way. The dramas of representing the sacred are constructed by the poet, knowingly, playfully, punningly, but they are also given, in the humbling, traitorous, unsaying that language performs. Even the poet—or perhaps especially the poet who grabs at authority and certitude, is unsaid in this context. And of course, so is the critic.

The most famous of Murray's early poems, 'An Absolutely Ordinary Rainbow', from the 1969 volume *The Weatherboard Cathedral*, can be read as an attempt to thematise this impossibility of representation. It is an attempt that entails both a solid, represented, vernacular image—'a fellow crying in Martin Place'—and the impossibility of interpreting such an image. The poem begins:

> The word goes round Repins,
> the murmur goes round Lorenzinis,
> at Tattersalls, men look up from sheets of numbers,
> the Stock Exchange scribblers forget the chalk in their hands,
> and men with bread in their pockets leave the Greek Club:
> There's a fellow crying in Martin Place. They can't stop him.
>
> The traffic in George Street is banked up for half a mile
> and drained of motion . . .

and ends

> and many weep for sheer acceptance, and more
> refuse to weep for fear of all acceptance,
> but the weeping man, like the earth, requires nothing,
> the man who weeps ignores us, and cries out
> of his writhen face and ordinary body
> not words, but grief, not messages, but sorrow,
> hard as the earth, sheer, present as the sea--and
> when he stops, he simply walks between us
> mopping his face with the dignity of one
> man who has wept, and now has finished weeping.
> Evading believers, he hurries off down Pitt Street.[14]

14. Murray, *Collected Poems*, 24–5.

The image of the weeping man has multiple effects, but no-one can say what they are seeing, whether there is a halo, a peace, a retrieval of childhood innocence, an instinctual need expressed, a gift of weeping, an ordinariness, a self-sufficient dignity. So the impossibility of interpretation is thematised. But the central fact of the poem is that it wants to leave us in no doubt, that we have witnessed the numinous bursting in upon the ordinary: the rainbow. The thematizing or saying of the impossibility of representation is simply folded back (another of language's tricks) into the poem's urgent need to open a space for authentic representation. The poet, as much as the reader, is seduced into believing, even as all believers are imaged in the final line as needing to be evaded.

We are drawn in here by the seductive communal 'we'—'the man we surround'; by the realism of ordinary Sydney—Tattersalls, the stock exchange, the Greek Club, the traffic in George Stteer, dogs and dusty pigeons—and by the authorial voice as witness, pronouncing: 'there is no such thing' or 'I see a woman, shining'. But it is the incongruity of this authorial voice that is the give away. While the speaker is one with 'us', held back with us by the dignity of the man's weeping, trembling with silence along with all the other slick wits, it is also, like Blake's wanderer in London, so certain, so prophetic. Its certainty is there in both its denunciation of the misinterpreters—'some will say, in the years to come, a halo / or force stood around him. There is no such thing',[15]—and also in its sureness about the meaning beyond words to which it is witness: '. . . the weeping man, like the earth, requires nothing . . ./ and cries out of his writhen face and ordinary body // not words, but grief, not messages, but sorrow, hard as the earth, sheer, present as the sea—.' What can the reader make of such analogies—the weeping man 'like the earth' requires nothing? 'Hard as earth, sheer, present as the sea'? These are assured similes that flirt with failure of meaning as they seek to represent 'not words . . . not messages'. But equally, and contradictorily, these similes emerge both from a prophetic desire, and from a very human agency, speaking in words.

Curkpatrick describes the Levinasian difference between a theology that diminishes infinity and one that comprehends, at different levels, prophetic witness, which 'cannot speak of God, even if "God" is invoked as the authority in whose name one speaks'.[16]

15. Murray, *Collected Poems*, 25.
16. Curkpatrick, 'Infinity', 27.

> Therefore, a contradiction occurs in prophetic testimony—having been apprehended by the infinite, the witness speaks by the authority of the infinite, but cannot appeal to any further disclosure or endorsement of this witness beyond the prophet's own words.[17]

And this is perhaps doubly so for prophets in secular Australia, the land of skeptics par excellence. What we have in 'An Absolutely Ordinary Rainbow' is the thematisation of a weeping man who in the end could only say nothing and 'evading believers, hurries off down Pitt Street'.[18] In Levinas's intricate and nuanced language, we have a portrait of the complexity of 'Les Murray' grappling with 'the impossibility of the "infinite within" . . . a subjectivity that is "cored out" even as it is "nourished" by this lack through excess . . . [a] subject . . . apprehended, exceeded, and hollowed out in its finitude, by the in-finite within.'[19]

In a wonderful Murray poem, 'The Mouthless Image of God in the Hunter-Colo Mountains', the reader is once again presented with the mighty struggle between representation, naming, imaging, and a registering of the absence of God to the human. In a scramble through mad past-midnight suburbs and grunting barnyard cacophonies—dogs and dingoes, fowls and waterbirds all barking and hissing and flexing in their own languages—you (an unidentifiable but strangely Murrayesque 'you')

> . . . speak to each species in the seven or eight
> planetary words of its language, which ignore and include the detail
> God set you to elaborate by the dictionary-full
> when, because they would reveal their every secret,
> He took definition from the beasts and gave it to you.[20]

In its bizarrely humorous Dr Doolittle progress, this three-part opera for animal and human opens out into its full theme: 'spirit'. Up through the wisdom of animals, and through the singularly human activity of 'Laughter-and-weeping'. 'we are shattered by joy'.[21] In the environment of such joy, humans move beyond the language of rationality alone, and beyond mere human emotions we may enter the place of 'the spasm which . . . turns our face awry, / contorts speech, shakes the body, and makes our

17. Curkpatrick , 'Infinity', 27.
18. Murray, *Collected Poems*, 25.
19. Levinas, cited in Curkpatrick, 'Infinity', 23.
20. Murray, *Collected Poems*, 184–85.
21. Murray, *Collected Poems*, 185.

eyelids liquefy.' In this place 'learned words bubble off us', and we are sung 'as a summer dawn sings a magpie'. If we enter this place, the detritus of mere human language drops away and we find ourselves 'exposed to those momentary heavens'.

It is a truly strange, exhilarating linguistic performance, 'The Mouthless Image of God in the Hunter-Colo Mountains': possibly a modern, rural version of Pentecost; possibly a charismatic seizure by the spirit; or an orgasmic experience of laughter and tears and liquefaction; a representation of the organic: animal, human and God reunited; but certainly an attempt in long, complex, often gorgeously rough hewn syntax, to claim a place beyond language. Or to speak in an other language—visionary, embodied, joyous, and way, way beyond the simple world of cause and effect, work and striving. It is something given.

This then is Murray's glory, his letting go, his self-contradictoriness, so much repudiation of human language, in human language. In reading poems like 'The Mouthless Image of God', this reader wants to cry 'Yes!' For all Murray's provocations, his sermons and dogmatising, his setting up of straw enemies, and his fighting words elsewhere, it is when this poet is able and willing to let go, to bathe in his own contradictoriness, and not to flaunt his pomposities and prophetic knowingness, that the reader too has a chance to join in, to receive the gift. 'The Mouthless Image of God' seems alive to all its own contradictions: a fully embodied and embodying poetry which is simultaneously envisaging a release from mere body; a language set to speak in the tongues of humans and angels and animals, while still needing to repudiate the failures of human language--dictionary-full, defining, logical, needing release into a place where there might be 'expressing repletion and bestowing it,' 'far from class hatred'. The poem seems aware of 'the impossibility of the "infinite within"'. In fact it rings with amazement at how humans so often miss the point—'playing the fool. / behind your arch will'—working for joy, denying it, deaf to the raucous, ridiculous, passionate chorus of creation.

Is language capable of representing (embodying, incarnating) the sacred? This essay has been arguing that Murray in a number of ways seeks to answer this question. For this reader, at least, the most inspiring, the most contagious Murray poetry, is that which does not insist on its own knowledge of the place, the time, the enemies and the friends of the sacred. For Levinas, the 'said' as the predicting grammar of the word 'God' must constantly be unsaid in order to bear witness to the infinite. For Scott, such unsaying is akin to an awareness of 'the precariousness of our own sacred contexts, the historical accident of our own sacred locations [. . .] in a heightened awareness of the relativity of all locatedness, human or divine.' In Murray's finest poetry there is this awareness, a coming to realise that it is impossible to speak of God, even as God is represented, imaged, mimicked, and called on. Such a realising, undone and done over again, is not a failure, but the very closest the poetry comes to the sacred.

Works Cited

Bolton, Ken. *Untimely Meditations And Other Poems* (Adelaide: Wakefield Press, 1997.

Curkpatrick, Stephen. 'Infinity, Insomnia and the (im)possibility of Theology', in *Pacifica* 17/1 (2004): 15–35.

Griffith, Michael, and Tulip, James, editors. *Spirit of Place: Source Of The Sacred?* (Sydney: Berget, 1998).

Kane, Paul. 'Les Murray and Poetry's Otherworld', in *Australian Poetry: Romanticism And Negativity* (Cambridge: Cambridge University Press, 1996).

Levinas, Emmanuel. *Otherness Than Being; Or, Beyond Essence*, translated by Alphonso Lingis (Boston: Hague, 1991).

Murray, Les. *Collected Poems* (North Ryde: Angus & Robertson, 1991).

--*Persistence in Folly: Selected Prose Writings* (Sydney: Angus & Robettson, 1984).

Scott, Jamie S. 'Geographies Of The Sacred And Post-colonial Literatures', in *Spirit Of Place: Source Of The Sacred?*, edited by Griffith, Michael and Tulip, James (Sydney: Berget, 1998).

Chapter Four

Tim Winton: *Dirt Music* and Dreams of Renewal

The 2001 Miles Franklin and the NSW Premiers Award judges obviously appreciated Tim Winton's novel *Dirt Music*, as indeed did the 2002 Booker judges in their shortlisting. And it is not hard to say why, at a basic level. It has all the elements of popular literary romance—thwarted lovers, deep personal struggle and a last minute reunion of a promising kind. Satisfying and popular, *Dirt Music* is a Neo-Romantic novel. Steeped in the rugged frontier landscape of the far north Western Australian coastline and the Kimberly, it presents laconic, hard or distant male characters (Australianised Heathcliffe's, both Jim and Luther), and a strong, passionate woman (an Australianised and arguably feminist-influenced Cathy, in the character of Georgie). And it provides a satisfying, if somewhat mysterious ending.

Further, in interviews about *Dirt Music*, Tim Winton represents his authoriship and his work in fully-fledged Romantic discourse:

> I had a novel inside the manuscript, but I didn't have the novel . . . It was a horrible feeling. It's what I imagine it must be like on the eve of your wedding to realize she's not for you, and that you'll have to suck it up to break the news to her, to everybody, that the wedding's off. I lay awake all night sweating, woke up at two in the morning, went to my office and started from scratch, writing the story out by hand. I got home sometime the next evening, slept for four hours, and then did the same thing again. I spent fifty-five days and nights that way. I had to get it done.[1]

Here we have the Romanticised author as hero—sleepless, working by hand, fifty-five days and nights, achieving his goal: the real thing, the real novel. And from the same interview:

1. Hogan, http://www.beatrice.com/interviews/winton/

> I can only do the one thing; it's all I've ever done and I'll just stick to that . . . I was ten when I made the decision to be a writer. It's been more of a blessing than a curse. I had one idea in my life, and I've stuck with it. The more people told me it was impossible, the more I liked it, the more I decided to tough it out.[2]

It is the wonderful, winning Australianised Romantic—colloquial, laconic *and* visionary, tough against the odds, prophetic. So, *Dirt Music* is a romance, and it is Romantic; and as I will be arguing, has much in common with one strong strand of contemporary post-colonial thinking. And this is where my theoretical interest in the novel begins, with an interrogation of what might be called the Romantic aspects of (some) post-colonial thinking.

Half way through the novel the central character, Luther Fox, this sensitive bush musician, full of loss and grief, exiles himself to the tropical coastal wilderness of Northern Western Australia, in a near suicidal attempt to wipe away the memory of family and personal horror. In his wanderings he comes across a cave in the escarpments overlooking Aborignal middens:

> . . . a wide-mouthed cave shrouded with rock figs. On the ledges outside the overhang are tiny dancing figures the colour of dried blood upon the yellow rock. He gives a little grunt of surprise. He examines the dynamic images, most smaller than his hands, and marvels at their tufted head-dresses and skirts. Many are weathered with obscurity.
> Inside the cave he sees other paintings in a different style. He stoops to look, but hesitates. On the rear wall a large mouthless face stares at him. Rays stream from its head . . . He thinks what the hell, and goes in crouched.
> The ceiling is taken up by a huge ochre figure in red and white. Its head is the size of a turtle shell, the eyes big and dark, and it too is mouthless. Arms like plucked wings. Between the splayed legs a strange trunk reaches down.
> Fox lies on his back to see it better. Such a fierce, staring face. Like a stormcloud.
> Hello, he whispers. Just visiting.
> The weathered face is twice the size of his own.
> . . . bright enough, the eyes still fiery.

2. Hogan, http://www.beatrice.com/interviews/winton/

> Halfway out into the light Fox catches himself making the sign of the cross and he stifles a laugh. Hasn't done that for a while.[3]

In *one kind* of post-colonial moment par excellence, the iconic guardians of ancient Aboriginal culture and a contemporary homeless white hero offer each other a blessing. Crouched and then prostrate, Fox's eye takes in the detail of these sacred, fierce, weathered beings, just as he feels he is being watched by eyes, 'big and dark', by 'a fierce, staring face'. His signing the cross is drawn from him despite himself.

What are we to make of this representation of mutual and beneficial post-colonial meeting? Fox has seen, and left unharmed, the 'still fiery' past; but it has offered its beneficence to him, awed and moved him, loosening him up. Does Winton succeed here in representing a fulfilling and even *transformative* cross-cultural moment, a meeting of indigenous and non-indigenous Australia, of past and present? Why does this fictive meeting leave some critics uneasy? It has something to do with the way in which it is almost *a picture postcard post-colonial moment.* At the back of my theoretical, as distinct from—though necessarily connected to—my novel-reading mind, I feel the weight of critical questions about the self in relation to otherness. Many contemporary theoretical approaches to such meetings stress not beneficence in the confrontation with the other, but the deep 'ambivalence of your desire for the other', 'the splitting of the self in any act of identification between self and other', to paraphrase Homi Bhabha.[4]

A literary comparison will, I hope, illuminate this concern further. I am certainly not the first to note the debt Winton owes, and acknowledges, to Patrick White. The comparisons between White's *Voss* and *Dirt Music*, for instance, are illuminating when thinking through this issue of self in relation to the other, across history. In an excellent article 'Land and History: Inter-Discursive Conflict in *Voss*', Diane Seaton writes of Voss's party of whites in inland Australia and the effects on them of the cave, also adorned with Aboriginal paintings, in which they shelter:

> From this point onwards, they have entered a new construction of time, one quite overtly emanating from the land and the elements themselves—and one . . . of increasingly multiple constructions . . . it is also in the cave that the expedition first comes in contact with

3. Winton , *Dirt Music,* 364–5.
4. Homi K Bhabha, *The Location of Culture* (London and New York: Routledge, 1994), 50.

> the Aboriginal legend of the snake . . . not only images referring to the world's creation, but those referring to the end of the world . . . if the Aboriginal discourse implies an engagement with time contrary to Voss's original desire to transcend time, neither is the native version of history at all like that of the imperial, European sense of history as inscribed in the epic construct, nor like those of any of the other characters: out in the unexplored land, still another discourse of land and history is encountered.[5]

Seaton is arguing that White's novel offers a complex and perplexed othering of the imperialising mindset. The resolution of the novel, and the white characters in *Voss*, is a tragic one. It is enmeshed in ambivalent, modernist transcendence, and a humbling, agonising confrontation with the unknown Aboriginal discourses of land, self and history. White's version of such a meeting is not the truth, of course. It is modernist prose. And it does make a salutary contrast with Winton's novel. Winton emerges in this comparison as a Romantic utopian, the purveyor of popular readerly satisfactions in ways that White does not.[6] A fuller comparison between White and Winton is needed to establish the ways that White's vision is just that, a mythologising and *bleakly utopian* writing of colonial history. But that's for another day.

Winton's writing in this novel displays his characteristic vernacular style, the combination of sacred and laconic, its dirt music. There is in all these elements what I see as his attempts at reconciling the psychic and cultural splits—between coloniser and colonised, between self and other, and between the genders. I am describing Winton as a late Romantic Australian post-colonial writer, a gritty metaphysician, seeking to interconnect the earthy and the numinous, seeing them in his immanent theology as part of each other. His works, from *Dirt Music* back through *The Riders*, *Cloudstreet* and *That Eye, the Sky*, and forward to *Breath*, share a vision of a suffering but finally redeemable world. In fact it is the suffering of the protagonists that is needed by the novelist to make the redemption believable. The plots of these novels depend on the suffering, as a kind of

5. Diane Seaton, 'Land and History: Inter-Discursive Conflict in Voss', in *Australian and New Zealand Studies in Canada* 4 (1990): 275.
6. Readers of Winton will know that other novels of Winton, the earlier *Cloudstreet* and *The Riders*, and the most recent *Breath*, for example, are not quite as utopian as this account of *Dirt Music* suggests about Winton. But I would argue that Winton's oeuvre is permeated by one strand of Romantic thought: a rich strand that seeks ways of representing sacred possibilities for renewal of individuals in the face of history.

redemption in process. In this way Winton's fiction is informed by Christian concepts of an immanent and suffering God, seen in characters who are simple, stripped down, punished and vulnerable, and finally purified.

Of course, looking at any traditional narratives, plots always have to be thickened, complications set in, sacrifices or horrors endured, in order that readerly satisfaction at the end might be achieved. Whether it is a happy satisfaction, or a tragic one, or something in between, all that *happens*—the fictional history of the protagonists—is traditionally *teleologically* conceived, always already at the service of the ending. And this is one reason why so much suspension of disbelief is necessary to read fiction. We know the end is coming, we are thrilled (if it is a good read) to see how all that has come before is trammelled up in what happens at the end. It is the inevitability of this teleological fictional structure that causes both pleasure for the reader, and my critical unease. It is an unease not about the potentially blunting, fact of these repetitive traditional fictional teleologies, but the fact that in the end such fictional worlds are vulnerable—politically, historically—for they are always finally recognisable as mere fiction, visible as part of the fiction machine.

In contradistinction to this impulse towards narrative completion, what happens if we work from the *poststructural* premise that there is always a far more profound loss—not simply a redeemable, Romantic, or even Modernist sense of loss—at the heart of all linguistic inscriptions? On the one hand, novels must end. Perhaps some scepticism, foreknowledge or blunting of surprise must therefore accompany any *theoretical* reading of novels. In an attempt at representing the processes, the splits and tears of representation, and their amelioration, vernacular fictions like Winton's are created, with their stitching together of ordinary lives caught between past and present. But if we listen at all to poststructural ideas, then Romantic fictions are still linguistic artefacts, and thus never able to overcome the lack at the heart of representation.

If we want to argue that literary fiction can be transformative, how do we address this post-structural claim that lack is what finally structures even the most utopian and Romantic representations? Take for example the representation of ghosts—remembered loved ones, lost in time; the ghosts of those who once lived in the land. Winton's *Dirt Music* is full of ghosts. We might argue that old ghosts still haunt happy endings, and that suffering—in real or imagined communities—can never be forgotten. Ghosts—not necessarily as perpetual victim, or angry rememberer of aggression, but the graceful, memory-full, sorrowing, open mouth in time—continue to cry out, unsure, unfit and unwilling to be fixed in language, no matter how powerfully transformatory that language seeks to be. A residue of grief and anger and refusal to resolve will always properly attend in human language, a trace of the force involved in making present what is absent, a losing hold of what is presented, in that eternal deferment of the sign.

But just what level or kind of haunting can readers admit? After all, loss and haunting are the very thematic stuff of Romanticism, always in the end recuperable, redeemable into Romantic mythology. In fact, they are a necessary part of such mythology. Post-structural thought is concerned with a deeper, more systemic loss. Perhaps an unutterable loss. A loss at the heart of language itself. As Bhabha writes, after Derrida:

> . . . the image . . . marks the site of an ambivalence. Its representation is always spatially split . . . it is the representation of a time that is always elsewhere, a repetition . . . the access to the image of identity is only ever possible in the negation of any sense of originality or plenitude; the process of displacement and differentiation (absence/presence, representation/repetition) renders it a liminal reality.[7]

It is fascinating to see that even in the face of this poststructural angst, its sense of the negation of any plenitude, Bhabha, along with many postcolonial theorists, can still be outed as a Romantic. This is evident for example in his essay 'How newness enters the world',[8] where he describes the possibility of 'an interstitial time and space', a living 'in the midst of the incomprehensible'. These phrases are tantalising in their implicit acknowledgement of the tension I am describing, as they manage to register past and future, the horrors of the past, but also the need to go on. And Bhabha *does go on* to describe this space, as he calls it, this 'continua of transformation', in more Romantic terms:

> . . . History's intermediacy poses the future . . . as an open question. It provides an agency of initiation that enables one to possess again and anew . . . the signs of survival, the terrain of other histories, the hybridity of cultures.[9]

7. Homi K Bhabha, *The Location of Culture*, 51.
8. Homi K Bhabha, *The Location of Culture*, 212–35.
9. Homi K Bhabha, *The Location of Culture*, 235.

There are quite fascinating Romantic, and potentially *colonising*, metaphors here. To 'possess again and anew . . . the terrain', signs that can be read hopefully, hybridities that enable.

In a by now canonical text of post-colonial literary studies, *The Empire Writes Back*, its authors wrote in 1989:

> . . . although, on the surface, post-colonial texts may deal with division of race and culture which are apparently obdurately determined, each text contains the seeds of 'community' which, as they germinate and grow in the mind of the reader, crack asunder the apparently inescapable dialectic of history.[10]

In this early post-colonial theoretical text, the seeds of a debate that is contemporary for us in 2010 can be seen to commence their germination. Already the ongoing post-colonial concerns with history and transformation are evident. For *The Empire Writes Back*, the hybrid reality of cultures 'replaces a temporal lineality with a spatial plurality'.[11] The volume is concerned with literary writers and their attempts to 'construct a future', 'a hybridised and syncretic view of the modern world'.[12] *The Empire Writes Back* champions, for example, Derek Walcott's vision of a '"historyless" world, where a fresh but not innocent "Adamic" naming of place provides the writer with inexhaustible material and the potential of a new, but not naïve, vision'.[13]

What is called for by the authors of *The Empire Writes Back* is vision, but certainly not naivety; history but with a hope of historylessness; the power to name, but never innocently. But is this another mode of innocence *recaptured*, one which has learned its lesson, taken stock of the losses, and now wants to begin again. New Zealand critic Linda Hardy writes in an excellent article on post-colonial poetics, of

> The utopian or idealist moment that authenticates a European presence in Australasia . . . the epiphany which has always been the modernist subject's dubiously innocent mode of entry into a 'new world', the 'settler dream of an originary innocence'.[14]

10. Bill Ashcroft, Gareth Griffiths and Helen Tiffin, *The Empire Writes Back: Theory and Practice in Post-Colonial Literatures* (London and New York: Routledge, 1989), 35.
11. Ashcroft, Griffiths and Tiffin, *The Empire Writes Back*, 36.
12. Ashcroft, Griffiths and Tiffin, *The Empire Writes Back*, 37.
13. Ashcroft, Griffiths and Tiffin, *The Empire Writes Back*, 34–35.
14. Linda Hardy, 'Natural Occupancy', in *Asian and Pacific Inscriptions: Identities, Ethnici-*

My argument is that the current debate amongst post-colonial scholars, evident also in various forms in the fiction and poetry of many writers, including Tim Winton, is one over how much history can be borne, and over how much history can be made, and remade. Do the ghosts, thematic or theoretical, prepare us for the possibility of transformation and renewal, or undermine any such possibility? In this debate, the tension is between what I would describe as Romantic, even utopian impetuses, and a less future-looking, freighted, and much bleaker account of history.

Undoubtedly belonging to the bleaker school is David Punter's critical volume *Postcolonial Imaginings: Fictions of a New World Order*. Deploring what he sees as the

> . . . triumphalist stance of the (post-colonial) theorist, (he wants) to break with the disavowal of pain and exclusion . . . and to re-encounter again the melancholy, the ruin and the loss, the ineradicable fact of genocidal violence in the past and the equally ineradicable fact of its continuation in the present day.[15]

The wording 're-encounter again' is rather poignant here, a double positive to ensure that the need to encounter loss is understood. Obviously Punter does not like the kinds of post-colonial theorising that he sees as forgetting the trauma and losing sight of the melancholy. He sees a range of theorists (it is a long list) as 'succumbing to the utopian lure'[16] and advises the need to 'continually remember to investigate the fictionality of . . . any "new world order"'.[17] His larger argument privileges the fiction writer over the theorist, as the truer post-colonial guide, in ways which seem to me to make the loss he is talking about into an overwhelming and unchanging presence.

In one regard I want to agree with Punter. We *do* need a cultural rhetoric that can remember the loss and violence, the overwhelmingly unredeemable facts of history. How can we ever think of forgetting? And further, in some ways Punter is right in seeing a utopic pull in the works of many theorists, a pull which can sound as if it is seeking to forget, to move on, emphasising empowerment, emancipation, agency and futurity. Some critics, like Bill Ashcroft, extol the processes of such emancipatory

ties, Nationalities, edited by Suvendi Perera (Melbourne: Meridian Books, 1995), 223.

15. David Punter, *Postcolonial Imaginings: Fictions of a New World Order* (Edinburgh: Edinburgh University Press, 2000), 187.
16. David Punter, *Postcolonial Imaginings*, 189
17. David Punter, *Postcolonial Imaginings*, 189.

'post-colonial transformation'; others, like Homi Bhabha, working more from poststructural and psychoanalytic methodologies, emphasise the linguistic ambivalences of such transformations—in the processes of cultural hybridisation, mimicry and identity formation.

What is still the most slippery ground in contemporary writing—theoretical, fictional and political—in a post-colonial context, is the ways in which this tension, this attempting to hold onto both the 'defiles' of history and to wing it into a new future is held. What might they look and sound like, these rhetorics which simultaneously seek to hold a recognition of history's horror, together with an attempt to see how history might be converted into 'newness'. Is such a simultaneity ever possible in writing, given post-structural and postmodern doubts about any such redemptive processes?

One version of 'transformation' between Indigenous and non-Indigenous Australians has been championed at the political level by the historian Geoffrey Blainey, and the former Prime Minister of Australia, John Howard. Too much dwelling on the loss of the past is described by them as 'the black arm band version of history'. What Howard wanted, he has publicly declared, was 'practical reconciliation', certainly not based on any public, governmental apology to the stolen generations of Indigenous Australians. A very different process of transformation can be seen in formation of, and the responses to, the 1997 'Bringing them Home Report'. The report is a crucial attempt to form a basis for future negotiations between indigenous and non-indigenous in Australia around the telling of Aboriginal stories, by mothers, fathers, children, communities. Many Australians wept in shame and new understanding as the stories of cultural, linguistic and family genocide began to emerge. As with South Africa's Truth and Reconciliation processes, there is a deeply symbolic, narrative drawing out of past horrors as a basis for future negotiations. The Human Rights Commission hearings, which led to the production of the 'Bringing them Home' report, were a harrowing and salutary experience for many Australians, both indigenous and non-indigenous.

Are we convinced by some post-colonial critics' optimistic textual and cultural semiotic approach, embodied in Bill Ashcroft's claim that: 'the *transformation* of that material culture presented to it as "dominant" or "civilized" is a sign of a surprisingly potent and even gleeful capacity for self-fashioning in colonised societies';[18] or Ashcroft's description of

18. Ashcroft, Griffiths and Tiffin. *The Empire Writes Back*, 220.

Gloria Anzaldua's writing as '. . . the conversion of the nightmare into the numinous . . . the essence of post-colonial transformation, the location of an experience and an identity that is always pushing beyond itself. Into the horizon'?[19] What do we make of Homi Bhabha's more agonistic version of transformation, which argues that 'culture as a colonial space of intervention . . . can be transformed by the unpredictable and partial desire of hybridity'.[20]

Some would argue that the explicitly fictional world of the post-colonial novelists and poets is a more convincing site on which to develop a rhetoric capable of taking history with us into the future. After all, the novelist has at her fingertips a permission to lie, to fictionalise, to move identities and fates in desirable directions, to conclude history, or at least the novel, in the direction of fulfilment, newness, change. Perhaps we should envy the novelists, as Punter suggests, who are able to let the imagination fly. We give them permission to be utopian, but we are suspicious of the critic who does the same. Yet there is a sting in Bhabha's quip, in his discussion of *Heart of Darkness*, that novels end because they cannot bear too much fictionality. In this clever reversal of TS Eliot's dictum, the same tension between 'reality' and 'imagination' in the formation of culture and identity is posed: Can post-colonial cultures be genuinely new, based upon acknowledgment of, but also sufficient release from, the horrors and losses of history?

The last scene of Tim Winton's *Dirt Music* contains a catastrophe and a rescue. Perhaps even a redemption. Cradled in his lover Georgie's arms, Fox, this white man who has dreamed of rebirth in an ancient land, has come home, finally. Grabbed back from the claws of a near-death accident:

> He lies with his head against the deck and does not breathe. The sky is behind her. She's real. She's not real. The others have faces they don't seem to own yet Georgie looked at the martyred jut of his hipbones, the twigs in his hair, the livid ulcers all down his thin leg . . .
> She looks in from the sky. Eyes wide as a fish's. Real or not, he should breathe. He feels his lips split in a smile. Soon. There's plenty of time for that.
> Georgie saw his eyes roll back and his hips lift toward her. My God, he was blue . . .
> Well, said the guide. You're the nurse.

19. Ashcroft, Griffiths and Tiffin. *The Empire Writes Back*, 193.
20. Bhabha, *The Location of Culture*, 115.

> Yes, she thought. This is what I do.
> She fell on Luther Fox, pressed her mouth to his and blew.
> She's real.[21]

From a narrative point of view, Romantic (and romance) conclusions to novels, with their visions of plenitude, redemption, new beginnings, need to conclude. Yet hope and promise often linger, even in the deepest melancholic ending. This, I would argue, is analagous with post-colonial theorists' desires to premise futurity, to mark out a utopian cultural space of transformation—with a will to newness, communal and individual empowerment, refigured agency, even in the jaws of history. History becomes redeemable. Both novelist and theorist must impossibly finish, have done with, what came before, in order to reinscribe it with the future. Both emerge with *redemptive desires* built on the Romantic fantasy of the infinite possibilities of human imagination, inventiveness, change and a sense of grace, in the face of the horrors which impossibly must be transformed.

In her discussion of so called tear jerker films, or 'weepies', drawing on the work of Franco Moretti, film critic Linda Williams writes of the place of fantasy in any meeting with the other. This fantasy 'that is always too late (in the weepie film) can thus be seen as based upon the utopian desire that it not be too late to remerge with the other who was once part of the self'.[22] In the melancholic losses of Punter's post-colonial imaginings, in the more positive, future-looking impetus of post-colonial theory's syncretic self-fashionings and empowerments, and in Winton's wilderness romance, we can see different but linked versions of this fantasy, this hope that 'it not be too late'.

There is one final, open-ended caveat to this argument about Winton's post-colonial Romanticism: what do we make of a different reading of *Dirt Music,* of the novel as a *white* romance, the story of white desire for belonging in Aboriginal Australia? How deeply inscribed by the Aboriginal other is this novel? The white hero and heroine find the beginnings of redemption, possibly, but some critics have argued that this is possible at the expense of any real acknowledgement of Aboriginal presence in the land. Or worse, it is possible only through the repression of that other, greater set of griefs and violences to which the land has been witness. Much depends on the reading of Fox's sojourn in the land, and what he

21. Winton 460–461.
22. Linda Williams, 'Film Bodies: Gender, Genre and Excess', in *Feminist Film Theory: A Reader*, edited by Sue Thornton (New York: New York University Press, 1999), 279.

comes to know by being read by the land, as well as his meeting with the quasi-Aboriginal figures he meets. Are we able to read the beginnings of Fox's redemption as, in part, his learning to live in and through the land as both other and as nurturer? Does the representation of the white man's losses mirror Aboriginal losses of family, home, music, future. Or does Winton's fiction in *Dirt Music* usurp such catastrophic loss in its narrative push towards (white) transformations?

Works Cited

Ashcroft, Bill, Griffiths, Gareth and Tiffin, Helen *The Empire Writes Back: Theory And Practice In Post-Colonial Literatures* (London and New York: Routledge, 1989).

Ashcroft, Bill. *Post-colonial Transformation* (London: Routledge, 2001).

Bhabha, Homi K. *The Location Of Culture* (London and New York: Routledge: 1994).

The Bringing Them Home Report (1997) http://www.hreoc.gov.au/social_justice/bth_report/index.html

Hansson, Karin. 'Patrick White: Existential Explorer.' (Nobel e-museum website) http://www.nobel.se/literature/articles/hansson/#4a 2001.

Hardy, Linda. 'Natural Occupancy', in *Asian And Pacific Inscriptions: Identities, Ethnicities, Nationalities*, edited by Suvendi Perera (Melbourne: Meridian Books, 1995), 213–227.

Hogan, Ron. 'Beatrice Interview.' with Tim Winton, (http://www.beatrice.com/interviews/winton/) 2002

Punter, David. *Postcolonial Imaginings: Fictions Of A New World Order* (Edinburgh: Edinburgh University Press, 2000).

Seaton, Diane. 'Land and History: Inter-Discursive Conflict in *Voss*', in *Australian and New Zealand Studies in Canada*, 4, at http://www.arts.uwo.ca/~andrewf/anzsc/anzsc4/seaton4.htm, 1990

Williams, Linda. 'Film Bodies: Gender, Genre and Excess', in *Feminist Film Theory: A Reader*, edited by Thornton, Sue (New York: New York University Press, 1999), 270–9.

Winton, Tim. *Dirt Music* (Sydney: Picador, 2001).

Chapter Five

Forms of Memory in Post-Colonial Australia

> When we smoke the houses that our loved ones have lived in, and say 'Yenandi' in the old tongue, we're not evicting them . . . we're ensuring their whispers continue the journey . . .[1]

The poetry of young Queensland indigenous man Sam Wagan Watson takes many approaches to memory. In his poem 'the dingo lounge' there is grief and accusation:

> those of the brown-skin lycanthrope
> have merely become the forgotten offspring
> from the dark ages of the dreamtime
> the black man's beliefs
> are being swallowed up and regurgitated in foreign lands for a dollar.[2]

Wagan Watson has a high suspicion here for the memorialising business, 'the dreamtime [that] can be resurrected anytime/and found on the video store shelves'. He laments the pastness of his culture: 'the bonemen hav[ing] performed their last dance/and the shrieks of the black dingo . . . unheard in the night, ('the dingo lounge', *Smoke*). In this haunted and angry poem his muse, Morpheus, 'in his arduous attempts to dream/has taken to anti-depressants'. It is a poem which lashes out at the commodification of memory by both indigenous and non-indigenous. But the poem mostly laments and castigates the state of those indigenous 'shapeshifters

1. Sam Wagan Watson, 'Author's notes—conclusion, 170', cited at <jacketmagazine.com/27/rock-waga.html>. Accessed May 2, 2005.
2. Watson, Sam Wagan, 'The Dingo Lounge', *Smoke Encrypted Whispers* (St Lucia: University of Queensland Press, 2004), 52.

[who] skulk around the dingo lounge/haunted by the screaming engines of the machines of consequence/. . . as their numbers dwindle'.

In a recent paper, post-colonial critic Graham Huggan describes what he sees as the current 'gothic period' in cultural criticism, 'characterised by an outpouring of often densely theoretical work on trauma, mourning, and various aspects of contemporary late capitalist "wound culture"'.[3] This paper will explore the tension, inherent in much personal, communal and national remembering, between such 'gothic' responses to the very real wounds perpetrated by human beings upon other humans, and what I will be calling the *sacred dimensions* to remembering.

One way of approaching this tension is to think about the ghosts who haunt literature and memory. Sometimes they are invited, and created, by the writers who refigure them. Sometimes they come uninvited. Derrida in *Spectres of Marx* speaks of the 'untimeliness' of ghosts, and of the uncanniness and anxiety perpetrated by their non-appearance. Huggan, drawing on Derrida, describes such ghosts of memory as continuing

> . . . to haunt us despite the reparative work of mourning. In this last sense, they can be seen as anti-commemorative; for whereas mourning domesticates the past with a view toward eventually exorcising it, ghosts move freely between the past and the present, confronting us against our will.[4]

I want to press hard on Huggan's adverb, 'despite' here, and his term 'mourning', in the light of Freud's early distinction between mourning and melancholy. In Freud's context, it is not strictly true that mourning is 'anti-commemorative', nor that it is necessarily simply domesticating of the past, in contrast to the hauntedness Huggan prefers. Freud writing a personal letter to a colleague who had lost a son, said:

> Although we know that after such a loss the acute state of mourning will subside, we also know that we shall remain inconsolable and will never find a substitute. No matter what will fill the gap, even if it be filled completely, it nevertheless remains something

3. Graham Huggan, 'Travel Writing and the Uncanny', paper delivered at the Borders and Crossings conference, University of Melbourne, July 16, 2008. Personal correspondence.
4. Huggan, 'Travel Writing'.

> else. And actually this is how it should be. It is the only way of perpetuating that love which we do not want to relinquish.[5]

It has of course been open to long debate as to the distinctive roles of mourning and melancholy, both debilitating and empowering. Like his disciple Lacan, Freud claims a kind of rightness—'and actually this is how it should be', he says—in relation to remembering loss, 'that love which we do not want to relinquish'. It is helpful here to remember Freud's distinction, that '[I]n mourning the world has become impoverished and empty; during melancholia, it is the ego itself'.[6] These are rich words in relation to communal and national remembering too. Is the post-colonial nation necessarily *melancholic*, depleted perpetually of identity, stricken at its very root; or can we trace, rather, the processes of *post-colonial mourning* at work—ways of accepting and remembering loss as empowering, bringing a sense of the rightness of remembering—Freud's 'how it should be'—processes which are potentially linked to hope, of not merely remaining with 'wound culture' and an eternally impoverished ego?

If we are to address the hope entailed in remembering, it is necessary to examine what *forms* post-colonial remembering is taking, remembering experienced differently by indigenous and non-indigenous Australians, but also differently by individual writers. *Can* memory take on the form of hope: hope as arguably itself an equally haunted process, one which is informed by intimate knowledge of the past, but which threads towards a future not yet explicit? Huggan suggests that the work of memory produces a mourning which *domesticates* the past, while the present needs to continue being haunted by ghosts 'against our will'. However, is there a possibility of *remembering* which does not simply domesticate the past, but which continues to acknowledge the past's potency and woundedness, *and* which simultaneously empowers us to imagine an unknown future? Is this a communal—dare I say *national*—form of remembering, or is it possible finally only at the personal, psychic level? (This is, I believe, the very same personal *and* institutional question about memory being asked in the recent papal visit to Australia for world youth day, in relation to the victims of sexual abuse by religious clergy).

The text of the Australian Federal Government's *Apology to the Stolen Generations* was presented in Federal Parliament to a gathering of Indig-

5. Ernst Freud, editor, *The Letters of Sigmund Freud* (New York: Basic Books, 1960), 386.
6. Sigmund Freud, *Mourning and Melancholia, The Pelican Freud Library*, Volume 11 (Pelican Books), 246.

enous leaders, and via a wide media hook-up to the nation on 12 February 2008. What does it tell us about current forms of remembering in post-colonial Australia? For instance, what do we make of the fact that the word 'future' appears thirteen times in this document of 360 words? *The Apology*, begins:

> Today we honour the Indigenous peoples of this land, the oldest continuing cultures in human history. We reflect on their past mistreatment. We reflect in particular on the mistreatment of those who were Stolen Generations—this blemished chapter in our nation's history. The time has now come for the nation to turn a new page in Australia's history by righting the wrongs of the past and so moving forward with confidence to the future.[7]

What can be made of the rhetoric—the metaphors, verbs and pronouns—which construct this symbolic act of remembering? 'We', that old homogenising term, is used throughout. Levinas would remind us that this collective pronoun automatically works its inclusiveness through *excluding* some; here the subject 'we' immediately sets aside the other as the focus of the apology, all those others—'the Indigenous peoples of this land', the Stolen Generations, those victims of 'past mistreatment'. This is not just carping on words. *Who* is offering the apology? The agent who perpetrated the 'mistreatment' and the blemishes of course: but then 'we' becomes 'the nation', 'the laws and policies of successive Parliaments and governments', 'We the Parliament of Australia'. Powerful figures, and impersonal and invisible at best. This collective 'we' is asked to '*reflect*' on the mistreatment, quiescent at best; but very soon, at line four, 'we' are asked to plunge into the future: 'The time has now come for the nation to turn a new page in Australia's history by righting the wrongs of the past and so moving forward with confidence to the future'.

A little space is left for mournful reflection, though *hauntedness* is not a metaphor here, being a more difficult public emotion. There seems arguably no longer any use, at least publically, for Freud's inconsolability, the perpetual mourning/remembering of loss (though of course that does seem allowed in terms of white diggers and the Anzac tradition). Some would argue that this moving on is appropriate, that the long work of re-

7. 'The Apology to the Stolen Generations', *ABC News*, at <www.abc.net.au/news/events/apology/text.htm>. Accessed March 1, 2008.

membering and mourning has been done and that, as the metaphor has it, a new page has to be turned.

From the opening line of 'The Apology', with its reference to 'the oldest continuing cultures in human history', memory is bound up with particular conceptions of time. The ghosts and traumas of the past are symbolically relegated to that past, as 'the future' takes over: 'moving forward with confidence to the future', 'For the future we take heart; resolving that this new page in the history of our great continent can now be written', 'a future that embraces all Australians', 'A future where this Parliament resolves that the injustices of the past must never, never happen again', 'A future where we harness the determination of all Australians, Indigenous and non-Indigenous, to close the gap':

> A future where we embrace the possibility of new solutions to enduring problems where old approaches have failed. A future based on mutual respect, mutual resolve and mutual responsibility. A future where all Australians, whatever their origins, are truly equal partners . . . [8]

Simultaneously the problems are seen to be 'enduring', but also to be levelled, all Australians equal partners. While there is much applause from policy makers, pragmatists, those wanting social justice NOW, for change and renewal, 'The Apology' has also been seen by *some* as a festival of white self-forgiveness which blots out the past and changes little; *and by some* as merely rhetorical, useless symbolism which changes little *practically*. From both ends of the spectrum comes a refuting of 'The Apology', and doubt that the past can be rewritten, or overwritten in this way, let alone the future.

Again, this paper is asking how hope can be constructed for the future if the past is held onto with *unremitting woundedness* and a concomitant refusal even to imagine possible futures. This unremitting grip on the woundedness of the past would arguably hold us not in appropriate mourning, but in the realm of *melancholy* where the ego—an individual's, a community's or a nation's—does not even desire its ghosts to haunt the future, but traps them in the past, or anxiously confronts them again and again in a present which can't move forward. What happens when we seek ways of desiring and allowing such ghosts fully into the future? Or perhaps we need to say *finding ways of accepting that they will confront us* since its

8. 'The Apology to the Stolen Generations'.

not a matter of sovereign agency here, either for individuals or nations. This would be a way of remembering, of mourning and of orientation to the future simultaneously. It is comprehensively not a linear model of time, history or remembering. In an interview Derrida speaks of:

> . . . a future . . . which refers to someone who comes whose arrival is totally unexpected. For me, that is the real future. That which is totally unpredictable. The Other who comes without my being able to anticipate their arrival. So if there is a real future behind this other known future, it's *l'avenir* in that it's the coming of the Other.[9]

Relationship to the past, to the present, and to the future is, for Derrida, anti-linear, full of traces which can never fully be recovered:

> . . . the rhetoric of memory . . . recalls, recounts, forgets, recounts, and recalls forgetting, referring to the past only to efface what is essential to it: anteriority.[10]

The traces of the past are turned to, of course, but we cannot be gods in relation to the past, we cannot invoke it as completely *known*. For Derrida 'limitless memory would . . . be not memory but infinite self-presence'.[11] We remember, we forget, we move into the future, we go on remembering. This is 'how it should be'; and equally, we go on filling in, substituting, but at best opening ourselves to a hauntedness which is the trigger, the provocation for deeply imagining the future.

This simultaneity of hauntedness and futurity can be read in some of the best poetry by Indigenous artists in Australia. Melbourne academic and poet Tony Birch has recently published a poem/prose sequence 'The true history of Beruk: [William Barak] (archive box--no. 3)', spanning the years 1835 to 2007, and invoking the presence of a ghost, the indigenous leader Barak, who lived in the early 1800s, along the upper reaches of the Yarra river with his people, the Wurundjeri. In the opening lines it is the white men of history—Cook, Buckley, Batman—and then a different kind of speaking by Beruk.

9. Dick, Kirby and Amy Ziering Kofman, *Derrida*, Jane Doe Films, 2003.
10. Jacques Derrida, *Memoires* (New York: Columbia University Press, 1986), 82.
11. Jacques Derrida, *Dissemination* (Chicago: Chicago University Press, 1981), 109.

'My Words', Beruk-Ngamajet--1835

Captain Cook marched--
in jacket and brass button
Buckley stood ragged
in possum skin at Muddy Creek
Batman came looking
with glass, beads, powder
and mirrors in a wooden boat
around the sea

Buckley spoke his old tongue--
the visitor is not ghost
he is not ghost
look at Batman's face
do not touch his skin
his bread or his house
do not touch his house

Beruk spoke the truth--
whitefellow shoot us
down like kangaroo
whitefellow come
by and by
and shoot us
shoot us down

whitefellow come
and shoot us down

The whole poem, with its prose and verse sections alternating, moves from this section set in 1835 to 2005, and we find a surprising, haunted and moving finale to the poem, as Beruk's ghost reinhabits the riverbed he once knew so well:

Beruk visits the riverbed—2005

Beruk moves quietly through the canyons of the city—all is stone still now. He passes the winking lights—imitating fife. He listens for machines grinding to failure. Beruk observes his reflection in the flaws of glass, now inhabited by the petrified few. Women offer themselves. Men spit abuse. While dead children drift silently by, on a journey from the river to the ocean. Beruk slips into the water, beneath the heavy metals—the leaching arsenic, iron oxides, poisons and the death throes of toxic fish. Below the monster hulls of ships the current carries Beruk onward and down, to where the riverbed of the Wurundjeri awaits his return. Beruk calls into the darkness—singing his travels until his feet meet the floor of 100,000 lives once lived. In the beauty and blackness of the riverbed Beruk greets his son, David. He then greets his father—the Ngarnajet. They sing, feet raising a rhythm of shifting earth:

we will be gone
all gone soon
we will be gone
and we will come
we will come
and be

we will be

Is this simply nostalgia? Memory struggling to hold on to what is passed, impossible, no longer potent? The fact is, in 2008 we **do** have the poem, with its images and voices, and we have the indigenous poet's will to 'sing, feet raising a rhythm of shifting earth', just as we hear Ngarnajet. and Beruk and David did. In an essay reflecting on his own poem, Birch writes about Port Phillip Bay and Melbourne, of

> . . . the recent dredging of the river—the Yarra River or the bay . . . Commercial interest, globalisation means that we're going to become a gateway city again in Melbourne and that we need to have a deeper channel to get bigger tankers into the port so that we can ship more goods into the hinterland as we would have said in the 19th Century. I was very interested when this dredging occurred, that in fact part of the exploration talked about the original pre-European Wurundjeri river bed, which is in Port Philip Bay and which exists today at about 115 metres in a ravine at the centre of Port Philip Bay . . . that Wurundjeri story which is deepest within the landscape . . . these stories reflecting contemporary landscapes . . . I do not want William Barak's story or the story of the Wurundjeri people to be a historical story. I want it to be a story that resonates in Melbourne today, so that we understand it

today. [12]

Past, present and future are haunted, *because* we are memory animals. The imagined/remembered figure of Beruk is one which causes us to mourn for a past of destruction and deep woundedness; but it is also a figure which finds shape into the future, 'where the riverbed of the Wurundjeri awaits his return'. Yes, there's mourning, and loss, and even nostalgia, but not the impoverishment of ego. Rather, the poetry enables active, imaginative, historical remembering, and refiguring into the future

12. <www.acmi.net.au/global/media/first_person_birch.pdf>. Accessed 14 June 2008.

Works Cited

'The Apology To The Stolen Generations' (2008) ABC News Website: http://www.abc.net.au/news/events/apology/text.htm (Accessed July 10, 2008).

Birch, Tony. 'The True History Of Beruk: [William Barak] (archive box--no. 3)', in *Meanjin* 65/1 (March 2006): 72–75.

Derrida, Jacques. *Dissemination* (Chicago: Chicago University Press, 1981).

Derrida, Jacques. *Memoires* (New York: Columbia University Press, 1986).

Dick, Kirby and Ziering Kofman. Amy. *Derrida*, Jane Doe Films, 2003.

Freud, Ernst L. *The Letters Of Sigmund Freud* (New York: Basic Books, 1960).

Freud, Sigmund. *Mourning And Melancholia,* standard edition (London: Hogarth Press, 1957).

Huggan, Graham. 'Travel Writing And The Uncanny', paper delivered at the *Borders And Crossings* conference, University of Melbourne, July 16, 2008. Personal correspondence.

Watson, Sam Wagan. 'The Dingo Lounge', in *Smoke Encrypted Whispers* (St Lucia: University of Queensland Press), 'Author's notes — conclusion', cited at http://jacketmagazine.com/27/rock-waga.html. 2004

Zehfuss, Maja. 'Derrida's Memory, War And The Politics Of Ethics', in *Derrida: Negotiating The Legacy*, edited by Fagan, Madeleine *et al* (Edinburgh: Edinburgh University Press, 2007), 97–111.

Chapter Six

Sacred Exchange: Peter Carey's *Oscar and Lucinda*

How is sacredness imagined in postmodern and post-colonial cultures such as contemporary Australia? Across the latter part of the twentieth century it has been a commonplace of cultural critics to situate the formation of 'Australia' at the limit of Western concerns about the sacred, or more specifically, religion. From the mid-twentieth century Russell Ward's iconic legendary Australian bloke is '. . . a hard case, sceptical about the value of religion and of intellectual and cultural pursuits generally';[1] poet James McAuley's Australians are 'hard-eyed, kindly, with nothing inside them';[2] critic Jennifer Rutherford's account of the reception of Patrick White's *Riders in the Chariot* declares:

> Not only is the religious thematic deemed un-Australian . . . Almost unanimously, the critical community has understood White to be exalting and idealising the four 'mystics' in opposition to a profane, malignant and aesthetically stupid suburban Australia . . . (this) attests to implicit conceptions of Australia as a site devoid of any encounter with those modalities of being that we can variously name mystical, sacred, religious or ecstatic.[3]

And critic David Tacey's influential 1995 volume *Edge of the Sacred: Transformation in Australia* summarises a common (stereo) type of the Australian identity, arguing that

> The loss of spiritual ecstasy in both white and black cultures has been replaced by the spurious, artificial ecstasy that is provided by

1. Russell Ward, *The Australian Legend* (Melbourne: Oxford University Press, 1958).
2. James McAuley, *Collected Poems 1936–1970* (London, Sydney, Melbourne: Angus and Roberston, 1971), 6.
3. Jennifer Rutherford, *The Gauche Intruder: Freud, Lacan and the white Australian Fantasy* (Melbourne: Melbourne University Press, 2000), 193.

> alcohol and drugs. We can all get drunk together, and then have a bloody good fight at the end of it: this is one of the few forms of shared social ritual we still have left today.[4]

Reinforcing such stubborn national stereotypes, the dominant postmodern and post-colonial critical debates about such twentieth century writers as McAuley, Buckley, Murray, Wright, Oodgeroo, Neilson, Webb, White, Malouf, Murray, Mudrooroo, Carey, Garner, Winton, and many more have most often been embarrassed by, or dismissive of a category such as 'the sacred'. This is despite the fact that many Australian writers have approached issues of sacredness in multiple ways: as problem, celebration, trauma, tragedy, farce, fullness or emptiness; as Romantic, indigenous, postmodern. I am using the crushingly monolithic and inadequate term 'the sacred' so far, but one ambition of this essay is to open up a number of possibilities about how contemporary Australian writing approaches issues of 'sacredness', focussing specifically on Peter Carey's novel *Oscar and Lucinda*.

And how could Australian writers escape the urgent need to examine Australia's cultural life, past, present and still forming, in this context of the sacred? While the commonplace myths of Australia as modern secular state persist, the last decades of the twentieth century have begun to open out a dialogue in which such terms as sacredness, spirit, belief, and religion are not merely seen as embarrassing or irrelevantly archaic, but as urgent elements in new national and global debates. In Australia, as in other post-colonial cultures, the confrontations between indigenous and non-indigenous have had and continue to have powerful effects; and globally, the need to examine the hydra-headed 'sacred' has its impetus in the broader debates of post-coloniality, diaspora, religious fundamentalisms, and the effects of capitalism.

In Peter Carey's 1988 novel *Oscar and Lucinda*, a complex set of binaries are negotiated: England and Australia; Christendom and Indigenous knowledges; divine providence and chance; adult and child; sensuality and sacredness. Many of these binaries circle around the fragile and conflicted figure of Oscar, the believer who makes his way—bumpily, accidently, trembling—to Australia, and to a believing which looks equally like unbelief.

---

4. David Tacey, *Edge of the Sacred: Transformation in Australia* (Melbourne: HarperCollins, 1995), 9.

Carey's celebrated novel provokes a range of questions about how the sacred might be probed, imagined and languaged in a postmodern and post-colonial culture. For bible-carrying, pale-skinned, terrified Oscar sacredness is bound up with the terror of his unlikely, colonising mission, but it is he, unknowingly, who is approaching his own transformation, even as he would transform the 'savage' land around him. Ensconced and petrified in his glass church towards the end of the novel, Oscar:

> . . . drifted up the Bellinger River like a blind man up the central isle of Notre Dame. He saw nothing. The country was thick with sacred stories more ancient than the ones he carried in his sweat-slippery Bible. He did not even imagine their presence. Some of these stories were as small as the transparent anthropods that lived in the puddles beneath the river casuarinas. These stories were like fleas, thrip, so tiny that they might inhabit a place (inside the ears of the seeds of grass) he would later walk across without even seeing. In this landscape every rock had a name, and most names had spirits, ghosts, meanings.[5]

For Carey, here, sacredness is bound up with stories. Or more precisely, the processes of stories: listening for them, and to them; making and telling them; attending to their particularities, their tiny, earthed and fleshed realities. As a novelist, he is staking much on the multiple, ordinary, half-hidden, communal and redemptive processes of story-telling. As an *Australian* novelist, he is also obviously learning much from the land, from the story-telling of the land, about the ancient, subtle, embodied, indigenous elements of stories. These are lessons which Oscar is slowly made to learn too, just as he had, as a child, longed for his father to listen to his son's divergent spiritual and sensual intuitions.

Beyond his bumbling, frightened will to implement the abstract tenets of his religious calling, Oscar is revealed more and more, to himself and to the reader, as the frightened little boy caught in the maelstroms of history. His hellish journey through the Australian landscape, is that of a child—itchy, weak, bullied, terrified, obstinate—whose journey towards transformation had begun in his father's austere religious house: as he 'took the spoon and ate', tasting the pudding which 'did not taste like the fruit of Satan,', 'treasuring it inside his mouth'.[6] It is a sacred transformation which confronts him, a sacred which begins to take multiple forms and

5. Peter Carey, *Oscar and Lucinda* (St Lucia: University Queensland Press, 1988), 492.
6. Carey, *Oscar and Lucinda*, 12.

discourses, in a journey which might be seen to imitate the terrifying expedition into emptiness of that earlier colonising fictional hero, Voss.[7] The child eating the pudding experiences simultaneously the hard blow of his father's dogma, and the fruit which bursts with pleasure in his mouth. This central contradiction gives shape to Oscar's journey towards the sacred.

This sacredness—or at least Oscar's glimpses of it—is hydra-headed and paradoxical: it is there in his terrified and passionate independence of spirit wrestling with the abstractions of his (equally sensual) father, that determined striver after 'the pure and uncorrupted word of God';[8] it lurks in his call to a religious, colonising mission; and in his role as passionate angel of justice, bringing his 'hate-bright axe down in the middle of Mr Jeffris's glistening, brilliantined head'.[9]

But the sacred looms most awfully for Oscar himself, stumbling on his expedition into the Australian bush. It is here he confronts the possibility of the savage nothingness which might be his God.

> In a pretty clearing beside some white-trunked paper-barks, Oscar saw a man tied to a tree and whipped until there was a shiny red mantle on his white shoulders and brown seeping through his Anthony Horderns' twill trousers. His 'mates' all watched. Oscar prayed to Jesus but no prayer could block out the smell of the man's shit.[10]

We are faced here with Carey's simultaneously farcical and savage antipodean vision: of a colonial scapegoat in his 'Anthony Horderns' twill trousers', and of Oscar's impotent prayer. It is the sensual power of bodily suffering—the shiny red mantle, the white shoulders, the brown seeping through, the smell—that stands up to Oscar's attempts at prayer. It is a rabid, desperate prayer, not for the comfort or support of the victim, as might befit a passing pastor, but for himself, 'to block out the smell of the man's shit'. It is prayer, it might be argued, that is stripped of its redemptive aim for the Christ-like figure strung up on the 'white-trunked paper-barks'. Perhaps a child's self-centred prayer. In Carey's approaches to the sacred in this novel, but no less in earlier novels such as *Bliss*, or *Illywhacker*, the struggle to comprehend or even glimpse sacredness is carried out in a specific place, and time, and body. The sacred does not

7. Patrick White, *Voss* (Harmondsworth: Penguin, 1960).
8. Peter Carey, *Oscar and Lucinda*, 19.
9. Carey, *Oscar and Lucinda*, 480.
10. Carey, *Oscar and Lucinda*, 464.

operate as the antithesis of the material, or the body, but in dialogue with it. The farce lets in the body (the whipped and shitting man, Oscar's revolted senses, the suggestions of crucifixion); but in no way are the sacred dimensions of the Australian colonial confrontations diminished by this. They are heightened. One might even say 'Australianised'.

Where might the sacred be found, how imagined, in such a place as colonial Australia? This sickened, stumbling and frightened Christian Oscar, still clinging to the staff of his religious mission and authority, is slowly being led towards a clearing, an emptiness in which his body and its senses and drives must be submitted to other stories, other bodies, other histories. But what kind of discourses does Carey use/invent to speak about sacredness in *Oscar and Lucinda?* Is there merely emptiness at the end of Oscar's journey? The pathetic realisation of his own huge, colonising intrusiveness? What postmodern and post-colonial discourses are possible for imagining the contemporary sacred?

In a provocative 1992 essay, Christian theologian Rowan Williams summarises a range of late twentieth century propositions about the postmodern sacred, theological propositions influenced mostly by the work of Derrida:

> God is an 'effect of the trace': to speak of God is to try to put a face upon that which haunts language—what is over the shoulder, round the corner, what is by stipulation not capable of being confronted, being *faced*.[11]

Williams places writers such as John D Caputo, Kevin Hart and Mark Taylor as, in their different ways, addressing Derrida in order to retrieve or radicalise his work for the *via negativa*, making différance 'an occasion for "grace"'.[12] For Derrida, and differently for scholars in his train, Williams sees 'the clarity with which the sacred, the order of grace or liberation, is assimilated to absence, rupture'.[13] But Williams wants (as, I will argue does Carey) to unsettle any satisfaction with this concept of absence. He writes, beyond Derrida:

11. Rowan Williams, 'Hegel and the Gods of Postmodernity', in *Shadow of Spirit: Postmodernism and Religion*, edited by Philippa Berry and Andrew Wernick (Routledge: London and New York,1992), 72.
12. Williams, 'Hegel and the Gods', 73.
13. Williams, 'Hegel and the Gods', 73.

> What is thinkable is so precisely because thinking is not content with the abstraction of mutual exclusivities, but struggles to conceive a structured wholeness nuanced enough to contain what appeared to be contradictories. Once again: time and understanding belong together; language constantly remakes itself in the fact of what is not yet understood, criticizes itself unceasingly . . . we can indeed abstract to the trace of a perpetual shadow . . . but this shadow *can only 'appear'* in the historical process of making (communicable, communal) sense, in the 'following' of discourse.[14]

Williams has many agendas running here, not the least being a desire to resist 'the relegation to profanity of the temporal, the communicative, the implied devaluation of exchange'.[15] Williams' is a theology which acknowledges the larger Derridean claims to God and the sacred as that which is never finally or sufficiently knowable. It acknowledges the contribution of the human critical ability to abstract, to comprehend its own inadequacies and the inadequacies of language, in the face of the incomprehensible. But Williams' theology is also one which seeks to understand the place not only of the abstract, but of times, places, words and histories which are experienced—spoken, written, narrated, communally entered into—exchanged.

Williams' concept of the sacred is valuable in thinking about the effects of the final scene of *Oscar and Lucinda.* Sitting in his ridiculous, sublime, monstrous and beautiful glass church, for Oscar what seems to remain are words which turn agonisingly in a void. His church is no longer holy. His body is sunburnt, throbbing, infected, itching. His prayer has become a begging, a doubting, 'digging his nails into the backs of his hands'.[16] It is a moment of collision when Oscar's language, sacred and profane at once, is slammed hard up against the failure of language to communicate. For Oscar it is not Williams' moment of language constantly remaking itself, but the seeming end of language, language as the production of false signs, of human blindness and farce:

> It was not quite dark. Flying foxes filled the sky above the river. The tilting platform became a ramp and the glass church slid beneath the water and while my great-grandfather kicked and pulled at the

14. Williams, 'Hegel and the Gods, 76.
15. Williams, 'Hegel and the Gods id, 74.
16. Carey, *Oscar and Lucinda*, 510.

> jammed door, the fractured panes of glass behind his back opened to let in his ancient enemy.
>
> A great bubble of air broke the surface of the Bellinger and the flying foxes came down close upon the river. When they were close enough for his bad eyes to see, he thought they were like angels with bat wings. He saw it as a sign from God. He shook his head, panicking in the face of eternity. He held the doorknob as it came to be the ceiling of his world. The water rose. Through the bursting gloom he saw a vision of his father's wise and smiling face, peering in at him. He could see, dimly, the outside world, the chair and benches of his father's study. Shining fragments of aquarium glass fell like snow around him. And when the long-awaited white fingers of water tapped and lapped on Oscar's lips, he welcomed them in as he always had, with a scream, like a small boy caught in the sheet-folds of a nightmare.[17]

What do we make of this fictionalised personal history overlaid on a piece of colonial myth-making? Is the narrative's outcome to be read as comic, tragic, farcical? Is Oscar's fate, as so many Australian critics see it, a fitting end for the bungling colonial missionary in the Australian wilderness? Or is there space for the narrative's tangled mix of lyrical and psychological threads to move the reader to sympathy for a myopic and bumblingly naïve character caught in the jaws of history and its larger movements? All language stops for Oscar, as the water laps at his lips, and he turns, with his primal scream of fear, back to beginnings, or to the void.

This narrative moment represents a deadly embracing of Oscar by his father, by his God, by his deepest fears and doubts, possibly by nothingness. But it also represents an end to nightmare. His father's face is imagined as wise and smiling; Oscar, trapped in a tiny snow cone of glass and water, is taken away from all his bodily pain, attended by bat-winged angels. Are these signs of promise or terror? Of the great void awaiting Oscar,? Or are we, in the density and interpretability of Carey's prose, offered language-making which is in Williams' terms 'not content with the abstraction of mutual exclusivities, but (which) struggles to conceive a structured wholeness nuanced enough to contain what appeared to be contradictories'.[18]

17. Carey, *Oscar and Lucinda*, 510–11.
18. Rowan Williams, 'Hegel and the Gods of Postmodernity', in *Shadow of Spirit*, edited by Philippa Berry and Andrew Wernick (London and New York: Routledge 1992), 76.

This passage, and *Oscar and Lucinda* as a whole, cannot of course be contained within a category called 'the sacred'. As Williams argues, the sacred emerges in *the process of negotiation*, 'the historical process of making (communicable, communal) sense'.[19] This notion of how and where the sacred might emerge comes close to Carey's playful, relentless understanding of the processes of story-telling: exchange, negotiation, community; passing on from one to the other, getting it wrong, seeking an ear; terrifying, enthralling, seductive, convincing, partial.

So how is the reader placed by this final scene, this piece of the story within other stories: Oscar's, the narrator's, the multiple, half-heard stories of the land? It is possible to read the glass church as womb-like, a place where the polarities of this character, and of the novel as a whole, are brought achingly together, momentarily: Oscar, the English Christian gentleman missionary confronted ultimately with the exigencies of chance and arbitrariness; and by the possibility of utter emptiness. We might call this transparent figment, the glass church, 'choric', a 'dancing receptacle', after Kristeva; a divine space on the 'borderline between all polarities: being and nothing, idealism and materialism, sacred and profane, silence and language.'[20] Associated with 'the chaos of infantile experience',[21] Kristeva's chora is metaphorical birthplace and grave of the non-subject, the one who must acknowledge lack of mastery, dissolution of subjectivity, of self and other, emptiness, a place of ultimate humility, an emptying of the self in both hope and doubt. Oscar has created this tiny colonial cathedral, into which he has sought bumblingly and stubbornly, to drag and house his sacred, but as his little shrine splits apart to allow in the dimly perceived Other world—Australian flying foxes and sky and river and land—this awkward misreader of signs, this Odd Bod, is returned by Carey to where he has always been most at home, the place before language, before religion, the place of terrible rebirth where the sacred might possibly be revealed. What remains are the community of readers, and Carey's words struggling with wholeness to make a story, many stories. And exchange.

---

19. Williams, 'Hegel and the Gods', 76.
20. Philippa Berry, 'Woman and Space according to Kristeva and Irigarary', in Shadow of Spirit, 250–262: 256.
21. *Ibid*, 258.

Works Cited

Berry, Philippa and Wernick, Andrew editors. *Shadow of Spirit: Postmodernism And Religion* (London and New York: Routledge, 1992).

Berry, Philippa. 'Woman And Space', in Berry and Wernick, *Shadow of Spirit* (London and New York: Routledge, 1992), 250–264.

Carey, Peter. *Oscar And Lucinda* (St Lucia: University of Queensland Press, 1988).

McAuley, James. *Collected Poems* (London, Sydney, Melbourne: Angus and Robertson, 1971).

Rutherford, Jennifer. *The Gauche Intruder: Freud, Lacan And The White Australian Fantasy* (Melbourne: Melbourne University Press, 2000).

Tacey, David J. *Edge Of The Sacred: Transformation In Australia* (Melbourne: HarperCollins, 1995).

Ward, Russell. *The Australian Legend* (Melbourne: Oxford University Press, 1958).

White, Patrick. *Voss* (Harmondsworth: Penguin, 1960).

Williams, Rowan. 'Hegel And The Gods Of Postmodernity', in Berry, Philippa and Wernick, Andrew editors, *Shadow Of Spirit* (London and New York: Routledge, 1992), 72–80.

Chapter Seven

Contemporary Sacredness: The City Poetry of Vincent Buckley and Sam Wagan Watson

Vincent Buckley's *Golden Builders and other Poems*[1] is an important poetic experiment in its direct and exulted address to the city and to the sacred. The city is Melbourne, in which Buckley lived, worked and wrote for forty years. In the original volume, the epigraph to the twenty-seven part sequence 'Golden Builders', is from William Blake's *Jerusalem*, a profound and idiosyncratic yoking together of the corporeal and the sacred:

> What are those Golden Builders doing?
> Where was the burying place
> Of soft Ethinthus? near Tyburn's fatal *tree?*
> Is that Mild Zion's hill's most ancient promontory, near mournful
> Ever-weeping Paddington?[2]

Clearly, Buckley's poetic and prophetic heritage and license come from Blake. The closing passage of the poem 'Ghosts, Places, Stories, Questions', from an earlier section of *Golden Builders*, walks in Blake's prophetic shoes, and is an apt prologue for the sequence to follow, positioning Buckley's high serious response to his priestly calling:

> . . . When the bush burns to ashes
> I still must touch my forehead to the ground,
> because its radiance is in my body.
> Gods are vulgar. So are journeys.
> Ulysses sails to find a speck of blood
> in the newly woven pattern; Orpheus

1. Buckley, Vincent, *Golden Builders and other Poems* (Sydney: Angus & Robertson, 1976).
2. William Blake, 'The Builders of Golgonooza', *Jerusalem: the emanation of the Great Albion* (London: William Blake Trust/Tate Gallery, 1991).

goes down to find mortality a blessing.
I walk beside these fires because I must,
in pain and trembling sometimes thanking God
for what they give me, the few poems
that are the holy spaces of my life.[3]

Steeped in biblical reference, draped deftly in analogy with the heroes of Greek myth, this is the voice of a modern poet who nevertheless takes on a prophetic and worshipping role—'I still must touch my forehead to the ground', '. . . because I must'. In the stance of humility (some might argue arrogance), the poet prophet repudiates Gods and journeys, but sets out seeking both: his poems are finally held by the poet to be 'the holy spaces of my life'. Readers who cannot move with the poem's prophetic self-ordaining (and there will be many, supposedly) may understandably be reticent to follow the processes of Buckley's sacred quest.

This essay argues, however, that what one encounters in Buckley's poetry is as much ambivalence as dogmatic assurance. Amongst contemporary Australian poets there are those whose work can be classed as overtly religious, whose poetry adheres to older, transcendental models of signification, to language and things in intimate, sacred relationship; and there are those poets who have gone along with the post-structural and postmodern loosening of such ties, diving into the various streams of linguistic scepticism. This essay traces the work of three diverse poets—Vin Buckley, Les Murray and Sam Wagan Watson—and their differing responses to sacredness, particularly in relationship to the city as a place in which sacred and secular jostle each other ambivalently, sometimes tooth and claw. The essay argues that the contemporary sacred seeks to recognise and construct what Luce Irigaray has often referred to as the incarnate, 'sensible transcendent'.[4] But the contemporary sacred is also necessarily a processual and fluxive relationship with that 'Other we can never name'.[5]

The poetic and theological interlock dramatically in the opening lines of Buckley's 'Golden Builders', as the poet prowls the streets of the inner Melbourne suburbs of Carlton, Brunswick and Fitzroy:

3. Vincent Buckley, *Selected Poems* (London, Sydney, Melbourne: Angus & Robertson, 1981), 99.
4. Luce Irigaray, *An Ethics of Sexual Difference*, translated by Carolyn Burke and Gillian C Gill (New York: Cornell University Press, 1993), 148.
5. Mark Taylor, 'Georges Bataille', ABC Radio National, *Encounter*, 22/4/2001, Sunday 7.10pm, at <www.abc.net.au/rn/relig/enc/stories>. Accessed April 24, 2001.

The hammers of iron glow down Faraday.
Lygon and Drummond shift under their resonance.
Saws and hammers are molten, they flow with quick light
striking; the flush spreads and deepens on the stone.
The drills call the streets together
stretching hall to lecture-room to hospital.

But prop old walls with battens of old wood.

Saturday work. Sabbath work. *On this day*
we laid this stone
to open this Sabbath School. Feed My Lambs.[6]

'Golden Builders' is a synaesthetic symphony. Body and stone, voice and machine, the city and the solitary watcher are willed into multiple conjunctions. Muscled, loud, shattering construction and change are everywhere, but so is the possibility of holiness in the city. The poem works through diverse literary echoes—of Homer, Dante, TS Eliot, Blake, Yeats, Lowell—establishing a richly hopeful but clear-eyed version of the city, not as hell exactly, but as the place where an active vision of redemption must be sought or made. Christ's directive to 'the experienced' on behalf of 'the innocent'—'Feed my Lambs'—recurs through the sequence, and the poem at this level offers to find or make or be such nurturance. The heroic masculinity of Homer's Troy, the blasted vision of Eliot's 'The Wasteland' and Blake's 'London', and the ambivalent 'Meditations' of Yeats flicker through the fabric of the poem, rich models for Buckley's Australian city in search of renewal.

But 'Golden Builders' makes its own assessments of this city's potential for transformation. Throughout its twenty-seven short parts, the poem pivots on the ambiguity of its own hope: 'We have built these squares, these towers. Feed my Lambs'.[7] The reader is buffeted by both the hopefulness of this line, its belief in the culture and the power of the human city to make and renew itself, *and* by a correcting call to choose what is most necessary, beyond the incessant building of nameless squares and towers.

The figure of the city operates in a shifting, volatile manner. Amongst its detritus—its rats and centipedes, its many small deaths—'They are digging everywhere. From street to street/the sound stitches pavements to-

6. Part 1 'Golden Builders' in Buckley, *Selected*, 111.
7. Buckley, *Selected*, 115.

gether. The drill/ vibrates with the vibration of his muscles'.[8] Sound and flesh and material and imagination weave together in the poem's continuous efforts to liberate the divided senses, and the divisions between spirit and body. That it is a hard and irresolvable quest is clear in the many changes of register, from sonorous prophetics to chatty anecdote, from the loose change of memory to the deeply-forged memorials to the denizens of the city: 'she' who 'burnt herself to death./ Almost too shy/ to go and buy the petrol'[9]; father dying in 'a tangle of tubes, pipes, gauges,/moon-travel gear';[10] dogs sacrificed for science in the micro-biology building, 'scratch of claws,/seizure of feet, the gulping voices';[11] Easter worshippers moving with baroque order, with 'marble and sensual will';[12] Benno, Francesco and Marco not at home in 'this shit of a country'.[13]

The changes of register, and the multiple faces of the city, are calculatedly unsettling, producing a space in which readers, along with the prowling narrator, become less sure of the nature of the journey, having to read again and again for the tone and direction of the poetry. Sacredness is unstoppable process here, aligned to older notions of the sublime, both beautiful and awful:

> Within the cordons of air, the pavements
> are hot as molten air. Sun falls with an edge
> or, in the evenings, the lights hang open,
> all the crosswires glint, all the saws and hammers
> locked away, and the melt spirit
> flows from wall to wall.
> Noise like blasts of heat
> like a door slamming at midday.[14]

Is this a vision of hell—its heat and molten air, its noise and edge blasting the body? Does the 'melt spirit' surrender here to the blasts, shut out by the slamming door; or in its 'flow from wall to wall' has it found a fluidity and beauty in the spaces and quieter moments of evenings? The city is caught in a trance-like vision, poised, perhaps ready to topple, but equally

8. Buckley, *Selected*, 114.
9. Buckley, *Selected*, 116.
10. Buckley, *Selected*, 121.
11. Buckley, *Selected*, 123.
12. Buckley, *Selected*, 125.
13. Buckley, *Selected*, 128.
14. Part XX11, 'Golden Builders', in Buckley, *Selected*, 131.

longing for transformation. From the polluted and noise-crazed city of hammerings, 'the chop and change of the machines', and not despite them, it seems, arises the poem's penultimate, transporting moment:

> Clear city
> you let me see flame
> touch angle-iron to iron
> run sap between them
>
> knit, anneal without torment
> or speaking these flashings your voice. [15]

Even as the preceding sections had seen the pollution, noise, racism, violence and shabbiness of the city, the poem and its narrator *choose* (desire, hope for, envision) a 'clear city', an enabling and potentially divine city. If one is of a mood to condemn poets as utopians, blind to the reality of grime and decay, then 'Golden Builders' might be assigned, at this point, to such a realm. Just so, 'sacredness', if it is an orientation of mind which takes no account of the haggard bodies, the need, the dying flesh of the city. Yet to see this as the final effect of Buckley's poem would be to under-read the poetry, which both builds and stands back to measure the repercussions of each stroke. In the material and literal realm, angle-iron touching iron creates a merely physical manifestation; but this is also the poet's chance to glimpse and build signs into the material universe. Flames become sap, which becomes 'these flashings your voice'. Physical and metaphysical flow into each other, but not in a heedless nor merely idealising way. The *mortal* nature of creation, as well as the power and grandeur of the human machine, are in dialectical relation throughout the poem:

> . . . The jet planes
> sweat in the air. At every boom
> the mortar shakes out in dust
> and the trim stones lean together
> earth shaken from the root or marrow
> from the bone. [16]

It is in human choice—to build, to seek, to question, to long—that this poem founds its understanding of embodied sacred processes. Alongside

15. Part XX11, 'Golden Builders', in Buckley, *Selected*, 132.
16. Part XXV11, 'Golden Builders', in Buckley, *Selected*, 136.

those of the hero and the prophet, sonorous and commanding models of sacred authority, comes Buckley's lonely wanderer. He is smaller, weaker, less sure. After the grinding of city stone and iron, the nights and scorching summers and lost friends, the narrator is last glimpsed 'travelling/ towards my timber birthplace', his final focus '. . . my Lord's grave? His grave?' The arguably dogmatic tenor of Buckley's earlier poetry gives way, in *Golden Builders*, to a vulnerability and ambivalence. We are asked to confront in the poem's last image not the certainty of belief, a reassuring, eschatological God sitting in triumph in His eternal City, but the grave. The narrator confronts the possibility of death, but equally of resurrection, the use of the personal possessive 'my', referring both to 'Lord' and 'grave', is indicative of the unflinching, steely-eyed hope with which the poem is invested.

For young Brisbane poet Sam Wagan Watson, self-identified Indigenous man of Buddjalung, BirriGubba, German, Scottish and Irish descent, there is also a penetration of sacred and secular into one another, as the historical realities of time, of modern Brisbane street life and the sacred values and traditions of his Indigenous heritage interfuse. Perhaps 'penetration' or 'interfusion' are inadequate to describe the often violent, physical and political impact of Watson's lyrics. Like Murray, Watson uses tropes of the city in dynamic relationship to 'elsewhere': 'a fire-pink, burner-blue horizon line', 'the lark of min-min lights', 'this stretch in my blood', 'the arias of the dry season', 'a brief Warrego sojourn', 'curvaceous segments of road/ like black smiles and frowns', 'a landscape bathing in a varnish of itinerant blue/as if the sky has reminded the earth of loneliness'.[17] But it is probably in the city poems that the sacred impact of Watson's two worlds vision is felt most dramatically. Upon the streets, lounges, gangs and suburbs of the city—his childhood Brisbane—Watson practises a hybrid, confronting politics of indigenous Australian poetics:

> longevity a whisper in the wind
> as their numbers dwindle
> and the dark hours are stolen by the monsters of new:
> drug addicts, paedophiles and killers
> the spirits have almost lost their foothold

17. Samuel WagonWatson, *Smoke Encrypted Whispers* (St Lucia: University of Queensland Press, 2004).

the children of the rainbow serpent have no use for demons
scientific justification has rationalised their roles with prozac
and institutionalisation
the dreamtime can be resurrected anytime
and found on the video store shelves
while in the dingo lounge
redundancy and health in death escalates
the bonemen have performed their last dance . . .[18]

Watson's scene is the down and out gathering places of urban Aborigines. In the loose-limbed structure of the verse, its minimal punctuation and fluid rhythms, the power of anger and loss slowly mounts in the surreal 'dingo lounge'. The anger is against systemic degradation, institutionalisation, technological and capitalist horrors—'the monsters of the new', drugs, prozac, videos converting ancient dance and song to commodities 'regurgitated in foreign lands for a/dollar'.[19] This is the world of drunk and depraved Aborigines—'the children of the rainbow serpent'—who are depicted as victims, and often as also maddeningly passive: they 'lounge', they are 'sucked in', they have 'lost their foothold' and seem to accept that 'the dreamtime can be resurrected anytime/and found in the video store shelves'. Instead of dreaming they have 'taken to anti-depressants'. There is grief in the poem's representation of this piteous fall from the time of the 'brown-skin lycanthrope', the dreamtime and the bonemen; but there is also a prophetic anger which seeks to stir and enliven, even to redeem. The prophetic voice is able to dispense with mere fantasy, just as simply and adroitly as it upheld the beauty and dignity of the past:

there comes no stormbird to deliver them to another side
as they fall into the landscape of the shadowmead
and the faded memories of the storytelling damned.[20]

There is both political anger at the systemic causes of such degradation and there is prophetic truth-telling, a holding up of the mirror to these passive lounge lizards by one of 'their own'. But equally, the poem offers to stand up, to stir up new dreaming, to face towards new song. Like fellow indigenous poets, Oodgeroo, Kevin Gilbert, Mudrooroo, Lionel Fogarty, Tony Birch and Lisa Bellear, Watson addresses a double past, a double

18. Watson, 'the dingo lounge', *Smoke*, 52.
19. Watson, 'the dingo lounge', *Smoke*, 52.
20. Watson, 'the dingo lounge', *Smoke*, 53.

ontology. For Aboriginal Australian artists there is the past of oppression and the past of land, dignity, custom, storytelling, song. At the level of poetry, there is the need to confront the equally material and spiritual degradation of many Aboriginal peoples; but there is also the possibility of constructing new song which doesn't merely wait for the 'stormbird to deliver them to another side'. The grief of loss is not allowed to be the dying cry here, but the call to richly poetic, political and spiritual renewal. For the Indigenous dispossessed who are 'scummed in the beard of night// whistling through blackened teeth . . . a black singing snake gripped by the neck . . . ',[21] Watson's poetry triggers possibilities for change, even as it keeps the horrors of the colonial past in sight. What is called for is political change for individuals and communities, but also spiritual change. The spiritual and the political feed each in the surreal image of 'the night house':

> the dingles of branches paint the night house
> while the smoky residue formed in the hate of its past
> changes the shades of shadow
> from black to red
> as if Dante himself had tattooed
> the limbs of humanity, those who came here to conquer
> or as urban myth relates
> those black women who once upon a time
> had their babies in this yard
> before the bulldozers mowed down the birthing plain
> and erected the doomed foundations of the night house
> unable to stop
> the curses falling.[22]

'The night house' is a piercingly symbolic poem that works through both naturalistic and surreal techniques. The accrual of corporeal detail constructs a larger political and spiritual edifice. The house becomes the site of Australian history, the place of urban bulldozing 'renewal' of what once was 'the birthing plain' of black women; the place of massacre; a site of city poverty and the home for losers. This is a palimpsestic vision—of birth plain beneath the urban squalor and dispossession; a more than merely material vision, one of Watson's many 'demonic icons of irreversible history' which is the macabre inheritance of indigenous and non-indigenous

21. Watson, 'brunswick st blues', *Smoke,* 119.
22. Watson, 'the night house', *Smoke*, 124.

Australians. But Watson's skills are also transformative, as he probes beyond the physical, giving the past power beyond mere nostalgia:

> the sepia images of memory
> in a landscape formed
> along the blackened fringes
> of this sunburnt country.[23]

There is a self-reflexive interplay of genres at work here, and in much of Watson's poetry: a recognition of the power of nostalgia in representation—'as urban myth relates', 'the sepia images of memory', 'this sunburnt country'—but there is equally a gothic, macabre imagination at work—'it is not the smell of Sunday roast that lingers in the air/but other flesh'. The interplay between these modes of imagining produces a haunting, uncanny, layered poetics of history, one that cries out first of all for recognition, and then for justice. Where, the poem asks, can the sacred manifest in such dehumanising history? The response is that sacredness can only arise in the jointly political and spiritual openness to recognise history as constructed of human choices, human making and remaking. 'The demonic icons of irreversible history' must be seen and acknowledged, but there is also the remaking by the poet, the re-fleshing of what was.

In poems such as 'bone yard, south Brisbane', 'night racing', 'brunswick st blues' and 'last exit to Brisbane . . .' we find a postmodern, hybridizing imagination at work, giving flesh to past, phantasmic images of indigenous dreaming, constructing contemporary urban transformations: 'a jungle gym . . . a prehistoric beast/ribcage . . . or an arthritic fist frozen in protest';[24] 'the howl of our twin-cam war party';[25] Brunswick St 'a black singing snake gripped by the neck';[26] 'fringe- dwelling in white-light static'.[27] At a political level the poems are protests against a colonial history of demarcation, degradation and loss. 'Last exit to Brisbane' relives the class and race history of the city, with its Boundary St boundary, 'the limit/where the dark-skin were told -/ DO NOT CROSS!'.[28] Yet as with many protest songs, the lost life forms are given a potency and new embodiment, becoming a motivation for change. While colonial history is

23. Watson, 'the night house', *Smoke*, 125.
24. Watson, 'bone yard, south Brisbane', *Smoke*, 81.
25. Watson, 'night racing', *Smoke*, 99.
26. Watson, 'brunswick st blues', *Smoke* 119.
27. Watson, 'last exit to Brisbane', *Smoke* 142.
28. Watson, *Smoke*, 141.

ongoing, those many who suffered injustice are given voice, made to cry out for restitution:

> and even today, at rush hour
> that tar permanently keeps the scar alive
> and the dead languages buried
> to only escape in the bitumen heat-haze
> and fall on deaf ears . . .[29]

Aboriginal history simmers beneath the surface of the city: a scar is alive, the dead languages are remembered and can escape, even if momentarily. The deaf ears of the city denizens, which fail to receive the past, are not the ears of the poet (or of his readers, possibly); the poem becomes the means of a vital kind of memorialising, a setting free. In the young country of Australia, how are the ancient histories to be released and remembered? The need for this to happen cries out in Watson's still-scarred city streets, the memories held in tar and bitumen, in street names, and in those who have been handed down the knowledge. These poems reclaim memory as sacred process: first the remembering, then the willingness to listen and to act. What makes such a process 'sacred'? For Murray, and differently for Wagan Watson, the sacred emerges when the ethical choices are made to listen and to act in the present. What causes some to keep asking, 'What has happened here?', 'What can we *do* now?' 'What *are* we, in the light of this knowledge?' The willingness to continue asking these questions, evident in Watson's poetry, is being argued in this essay as part of a *sacred process* that cannot be reduced to merely material or political questions. Watson's is a haunted, new dreaming, an unwillingness to forget the ancestors and their languages, a desire to sing them up into the present world from beneath the city's bitumen and scarred terrain.

A political drive to tell his own stories of colonial degradation informs Watson's poetry at every turn. But there is also, in the often comic, raffish energy of the poetry a refusal to let injustice and loss stand as the final note, as the poetry broadens out into deeper registers. His 'night racing' is a cheeky teenage tale:

> hugging into corners
> accelerating into the straights
> a growling junkyard dingo under the bonnet;

29. Watson, *Smoke*, 141.

the beast made up from parts here and there
born for the walkabout rally
black feet pumping racing pedal to floor
breaking the silence of the settlers' sacred sites
enveloped in shadows when not haunted by the silhouettes of
urban myth.[30]

Urban Aboriginal kids, 'our small bodies shivering a *techno* pulse', growing up away from traditional family sites, find and make their world, trailing with them the snippets and skerricks of a past which they themselves only guess at—dingo, walkabout, sacred sites—even as they refigure it. Watson's transformations are incomplete sacred fragments, often irreverent and larrikinish, with the image of the highway—'the bitumen vine of wandering impetus' ('we're not trucking around',[31] predominating, as the various narrators move back and forward in a restless pattern of past and present: it is the highway which 'drove right through the bora-ring/ and knocked our phone off the hook/forever'.[32] But this highway is also infused by a sense of sacred temporal dimensions:

the encroaching absalom before us all
an electronic highway[33]

Watson's is a young, deeply historical voice informed with an apocalyptic sense of ongoing colonial debts to be paid. He clear-sightedly and prophetically depicts the psychic, spiritual and physical payments being made by Aboriginal Australians. But as well as the protests of such representations, Watson calls for a clear-sighted and listening *response*—not least from his readers—to the lives and dreams of contemporary urban Aboriginal Australians.

Vin Buckley and Sam Wagan Watson have been analysed in this essay as prophetic, working within and through what have been claimed as sacred processes. Prophets as a class are certainly not what contemporary Australian culture warmly welcomes, particularly if the laying down of mandates or moral dogma, or the telling of truths is seen as the prophets' main business. However, the very distinctions between these poets open

30. Watson, 'night racing', *Smoke*, 99.
31. Watson, *Smoke*, 91.
32. Watson, *Smoke*, 90.
33. Watson, *Smoke*, 90.

up wider possibilities for thinking about the contemporary, embodied and processual sacred. What is a prophet? The term conjures judgemental moral voices in the wilderness, alienated representatives of their people; or lonely individuals suffering deep dissatisfaction with merely political and material explanations, seeking without hope of earthly resolution and explanation. But prophets have always been harbingers of transformation. Poetry is arguably the pre-eminent form of writing which can carry the hope of (formal, figural) contact with the sacred, that 'Other we can never name';[34] a hope which simultaneously registers the incarnate *and* processual nature of the sacred. The city then, as a place of material and spiritual flux, operates in the poetry of Buckley and Watson, as a metonymic site of the *embodied sacred*, Irigaray's 'sensible transcendent'. In their city poetry there is evident, differently for each poet, a refiguring desire expressed in tropes of (risky, wavering, hoped-for) immanence: 'When the bush burns to ashes/I still must touch my forehead to the ground,/because its radiance is in my body',[35] 'the spirits have almost lost their foothold'.[36] What emerges are two different, related poetries of the processual, transformative sacred crying out for acknowledgement in the interstices of the modern city.

34. Taylor, 'Georges Bataille', 27.
35. Buckley, *Selected*, 99.
36. Watson, *Smoke*, 52.

Works Cited

Blake, William. *Jerusalem: The Emanation Of The Great Albion (*London: William Blake Trust/Tate Gallery, 1991).

Buckley, Vincent. *Poetry And The Sacred* (London: Chatto & Windus, 1968).

----'The Image Of Man In Australian Poetry', in *Essays In Poetry Mainly Australian* (Carlton: Melbourne University Press, 1957).

----*Golden Builders* (Sydney: Angus & Robertson, 1976).

---- *Selected Poems* (London, Sydney, Melbourne: Angus& Robertson, 1981).

Devlin-Glass, Frances, and McCredden, Lyn. *Feminist Poetics of the Sacred: Creative Suspicions* (New York: Oxford University Press, 2001).

Irigaray, Luce. *An Ethics Of Sexual Difference*, translated by Burke, Carolyn and Gill, Gillian C. (New York: Cornell University Press, 1993).

Murray, Les. *Collected Poems* (Sydney: Angus & Robertson, 1976/1991).

Wallace Crabbe, Chris. 'Vincent Buckley And The Poetry of Presence', in the *Journal of Popular Culture* 2/2 (Fall 1989): 81–91.

Rowe, Noel. 'How To Gossip With Angels: Australian Poetry After The Gods', in *Antipodes*, 19/2 (December 2005): 177–183.

Taylor, Mark. 'Georges Bataille'. ABC Radio National, *Encounter*: 22/4/2001, Sunday 7.10pm. http:www.abc.net.au/rn/relig/enc/stories

Watson, Samuel Wagan. *Smoke Encrypted Whispers* (St Lucia: University of Queensland Press, 2004).

Chapter Eight

'Untranscended/life Itself': The Poetry of Pam Brown

There are many ways to peel an onion: sharp knife and tears; under water like your mother taught you; surreptitiously, creeping in, layer by layer; or with sunglasses on. And cunning poet Pam Brown knows them all. There they are, those devastatingly onion-like little poems, with furled skins and layers, offering up biting street-scapes and cafés, half-remembered far-away places, distant friends, rock & roll, and lost, ordinary cities; that deceptive, seemingly autobiographical voice cruising between wit, boredom, disillusion, nostalgia, paranoia, irony. Always irony. Always the slippery poetics of knowledges warping, even as the poet obsessively scans the texts for narrative: a seeking of 'untranscended /life itself'.[1]

Brown is one of Australia's lesser known great poets, if great equates with being revered by her peers; appreciated by a growing number of academics; read by a coterie of fans; producing prolifically in her own minimalist way; being steeped in Australian and international poetics; producing work which is philosophically and technically rich; and being someone who contributes to the wider literary world through her editing, her mentoring of younger poets, her embracing and discerning of literary culture embedded in an always bigger, baggier world. Brown's works, produced over thirty years, are not widely available. They include volumes such as *New and Selected Poems* (1990), *This World/This* Place (1994), *Little Droppings* (1994), *50–50* (1997), *Dear Deliria: New and Selected Poems* (2002), *Text Thing* (2002) and 2005's *Let's Get Lost*. The latter is a collaboration between poets and friends Pam Brown, Ken Bolton and Laurie Duggan. At last count there were eighteen poetry collections, with several of these overlapping in a number of *Selected Works*.

1. Pam Brown, 'Patti Smith was right', *Dear Deliria: New & Selected Poems* (UK, USA/ Australia: Salt Publishing, 2003). Cited in *Cordite* no. 9. http://www.cordite.org.au/ poetry/music/pam-brown-patti-smith-was-right/

However, critical attention has not been extensive. Despite being highly regarded within a small group of poets and peers Brown has typically published in a scattered, small-press way. However, *Dear Deliria's* appearance with Salt Publishing should see her work better distributed. While this small-press, small readership approach is something most Australian poets know intimately, Brown has made it into an art form, and one which seems in keeping with her own ironic and at times cynical approach to the world of appearance, celebrity and media hype. Brown's career is very far away from such scenes, not it seems through self-effacement or a shy-poet-in-the-garret attitude. There is just a residual toughness, a pervasive, questioning cynicism, and a stubborn faithfulness to language's plasticity which Brown's poem's embody, attitudes which seem to come from the deeper registers of this poet's intellectual and artistic life as it is lead in contemporary Australia.

Reviewers describe Brown as a satirist, as improvisational, wittily paranoid and world-weary, ironic. She is, and does, all these things in her poem 'Flickering Gaudi' from the 1994 volume *This World. This Place.*

> What to drink in remembrance of friends, of ideas, of projects, of eight millimetre films, of sketchbooks, screenprints, letters all eliding somehow in the depths of the pile?
> The extemporary verve of designs for a life which never evolve into actual manufacture. And now, in a kind of inner-suburban isolation, brilliant—bright—paintings are attentively wrapped & stacked at the back of a wardrobe. Mild domesticity where reasonable evenings become numinous nights of reading difficult books patiently flat on your back & raging, privately, laughing, noting the clues, improving your vocabulary, never your method.[2]

There is indeed improvisation—of a careful, knowing kind—in the eclectic tumble of things and moods, moments of brief existential measuring: 'a kind of inner-suburban/isolation', 'Mild domesticity', 'reasonable evenings', 'on your back & raging'. The wonderful swing of 'The extemporary verve of designs for a life' threatens to quite undo the aim of this essay. The poem's continual riffing on ephemerality—the life never evolving 'into actual manufacture', or realised method—offers a challenge to this reader, both to go with the quizzical, self-deprecating wit of the surface, and to stake a claim *about depth* in this wonderfully extemporizing poetry.

2. Brown, Pam, *This World. This Place* (St Lucia, Brisbane: University of Queensland Press, 1994), 100–101.

In the poem 'Scenes', from the 2002 volume *Text Thing*, Brown is still concertedly at these meditations on detritus.

> that white plastic bag
> has been drifting
> from the gutter
> to the road
> for three days,
> when the rainwater
> carries it off
> to the Tasman Sea
> I think I'll miss it.[3]

One of the intriguing things about this scene from 'Scene' is its careful noting: of place, colour, time, destination and feeling. Such care is at odds, hauntingly, with the transient nature of the observation. But there is also a poignant realisation in the understatedness of the poem, that the things of the world are intimately connected to emotions, or at least the observer continues to make the connection, albeit tentatively: 'I think I'll miss it'" The scene is reminiscent of the film *American Beauty*, as the young druggy stands mesmerised by the plastic bag lifting and falling in gusts of wind. Just why that film scene was so moving is hard to explain—did it present an image of transience? A glimpse of nature in a ferociously human world? Of forces outside human power? In both the film and the poetry scenes can be found the link to something faintly glimpsed, so ironically distanced and understated, that is nevertheless my clue in turning to an interpretive reading of Pam Brown's work.

However admiring I am of the spare, sharp, witty and ironic poetry of Brown, turning on its recurrent tropes of ephemerality, memory, place and postmodern subjectivity, this essay will move beyond admiration. It will read *against the grain* of Brown's own urbane secularity, with its emphases on transience, distance, its critique of lack of depth in the modern world, arguing for a reading of Brown's works within a category of sacredness. This is indeed an uphill argument, one by which I imagine Brown, the poet of 'untranscended life/itself', would be bemused. In this climb I will call on the work of early twentieth century sociologist, novelist and secular theologian Georges Bataille, and his anti-institutional and transgressive concepts of the sacred. Further, the essay will confront ideas

3. Pam Brown, *Text Thing* (Adelaide: Little Esther Books, 2002), 130–132.

about the sacred in Brown's familiar haunt, the city, so often the icon of godlessness, whether it be in the guise of disenchanted, secular modernity, the technological, commercial, chartered place; or differently, as the place of decadence, Sodom and Gomorrah. Within this context, here is the opening of Brown's poem 'Pique', from her 1997 volume *50–50:*

no one
on the corner
here

silent,
not spiritual,
the city is empty

antispectacular
& as
deodorised
as heaven

no sleeping boys
no density
no belching
pissing bodies
no spitting
in the street

utilitarian –
  make one step
    another step
        follows

the pace set
  by the tedium
      of the blessed[4]

There's so much going on in these seemingly laconic and wittily spare little lines, though 'sacredness' is not what the poem appears to be focussed upon; quite the opposite, it seems. Brown's poetry could be described as wry, postmodern, jauntily profane, captured in the little dance of 'Pique', with its stepped out little rhythms and sharp observational city-scapes.

4. Pam Brown, *50–50* (Adelaide: Little Esther Books, 1997), 67–68.

So where do I hope to get in fretting away at the categories of sacred and profane? In his essay 'Savage Metropolis', critic Andrew McCann argues, through a reading of Australian colonial aesthetics, and of Marcus Clarke in particular, 'that modernity brings with it a degree of regret related to its disenchantment'.[5] He argues of Clarke's view:

> In a world where cultural authority resided increasingly with the agents of technological and scientific progress . . . pre-modern 'belief in sacred incarnations, in heavenly interpositions, in personal relations with the awful Spirit of the Universe, is dead' [Clarke's words] the 'creed of the nineteenth century' is unambiguously secular.[6]

Despite this claim to secularity, in McCann's argument Modernity's regret about its own disenchantment in Australia informs a larger repressed colonial sense of the *uncanny* which arose, again and again seeking pleasure in the *animistic*, in the very things it was meant to be so far beyond. Further, he argues that 'the rituals of a "dead and forgotten creed"'—and here he is referring specifically to colonial responses to *Indigenous* beliefs and practices—are located 'inside the Western Imagination'.[7]

If we accept McCann's argument that colonial writers and readers such as Marcus Clarke are caught in the gap between modern disbelief in the old creeds and superstitions, and nineteenth-century readerly and writerly predilections for the gothic, the barbaric ritual, the eroticised, indigenous sacred, surely the post-colonial, poststructurally-informed writer, such as Pam Brown, is several steps beyond this—aware of these colonial, racial and cultural blindnesses, but self-reflexive too of language as the site most complicit in constructing such blindnesses. After all, Derrida demonstrates the logocentricity of language, the ways in which indicators of sacred beliefs—truth, centre, God—cannot be eradicated, but can be constantly questioned and displaced, revealed in their internal difference. Looking back at modernity's ambivalent attempts to dispel the sacredness of the word, and looking around at the poststructural word which knows it will betray itself, and at the post-colonial word which tries but cannot open itself up *enough* to alterity, what can a poet do? Where can she go?

5. Andrew McCann, 'Savage Metropolis: Animism, Aesthetics and the Pleasures of a Vanished Race', in *Textual Practice* 17/2 (2003): 325.
6. McCann, 'Savage Metropolis', 325.
7. McCann, 'Savage Metropolis', 330.

I want to suggest several ways in which Brown's poetry of the city is a poetry readable within the context of the sacred, a category which gives full play to such directional questions. The first indication of this is when we look at Brown's uses of irony. Of Bataille's work on the sacred, critic Jean Michel Heimonet writes that the function of irony 'is to 'torture' discourse, to empty it of positive content by pressing it up against a blind spot, a symbolic no-man's-land that simultaneously reveals to the discourse its own finitude and its beyond'.[8]

And this is partly what Brown's ironic, throw away lines are engaged in doing: a constant confronting of the finitude of discourse which, it is argued, is at the same time a desire for the 'beyond' of discourse. The city of 'Pique' is empty, silent, unspectacular. Here there is even the asserted *absence of abjection*: in Brown's city there is 'no belching/ pissing bodies/ no spitting'—although of course her words are necessarily bodying forth the very thing they seek to negate. She plays here with the limits of her own discourse—its lack of spectacle, density; its repeated rhythms, just like the tedium of the blessed. And goodness knows who these blessed are—the saints of old going about their ritual, circumscribed duties perhaps? Or those who are unreflectively happy, seemingly unlike the narrator of the poem? And all the poet can do is mimic and ironise such tedium and emptiness, her little step down lines making a mockery of the rituals of the blessed, but also of the imitative artist looking for her narrative.

However, in part two of the poem another strategy *is* tried, as the poem constructs its comically red-neck, blasphemous vignettes. After the poetic hiatus of 'the pace set/by the tedium/of the blessed' we have constructed for us—in a seeming reaction to the tedium—an almost impersonal, visceral desire for

demolishing
  half the house
    to make room
for the truck

bashing the bricks
  with
    a blunt tang

8. Jean Michel Heimonet, 'Bataille and Sartre: The Modernity of Mysticism', in *Diacritics* 26/2 (1996): 63.

aiming
  the air rifle
    anywhere

blasting doves
      from
telegraph poles

shouting and strutting
    down
      BBQ lane

setting fire
  to lakes.[9]

What else can you do in the empty, silent, unspectacular and utilitarian city, but run amok, disrupt the silence, bash, aim, blast, shout and strut? In the vacuum of such a city, how to find a role, how to write, how to live? Well, one last thing you can do is turn the irony back on yourself, the poet:

& here am I,
  nibbling
    my jejune nourishment
with the laxity
    of a cultivated
      & singular minority
languidly
  erasing
    all legend

flick flick flick.[10]

Nothing sacred here—all legend (text and belief) casually self-erasing. Or is it? One effect of the irony is to mock the languidness of poet *and* audience, the 'cultivated/ & singular minority', that adopts the gesture of power, the eradication of all legend, but at the same time hails its own laxity and jejune cannibalism of the very thing it claims to mock. So the empty streets of the poem *are filled* with pissing and spitting bodies; narrative excitement is unlocateable, and mocked as the tedium of the blessed, *and*

9. Brown, *50–50*, 68–69.
10. Brown, *50–60*, 70.

comically whipped up in the violent acts of nameless larrikins (and poets). Language goes rushing in to fill the void it equally represents. So, the poet or the poem recognises, à la Bataille, that she is confronted by 'the finitude of discourse, and its beyond'. But does confronting the finitude necessarily issue in a 'beyond'? And what on earth might that be? Is it all that out there which refuses to manifest itself when you speak or write—and in this case *that which will not manifest* is equally narrative, spectacle, *and* the very void, the emptiness, the silence. Language refuses such silence, but is constantly submitting to it. In fact, I am arguing that this is Brown's recurrent theme: the impossibility of the sacred, and the impossibility of resting with that impossibility.

In the poem 'Relic' we read: 'what faith!/flailing & thrashing/beating dry bones/on rust-flaked drums/practising ritual/as if it were possible to swallow/an arrow.'[11] In 'Pique' the gap between the patterned tedium of the silent city and the random violence of bashing bricks, blasting doves, shouting and strutting down BBQ lane sets up an ironic interplay between what will not shine—the city as not spiritual, antispectacular, deodorised, one step placed dutifully or ploddingly after another—and the bizarre violence of language, or poets, seeking to force event or response. As if something was possible. Like Walter Benjamin's flâneur, the characters in Brown's poetry go about declaring the decay of aura, the loss of sacred possibility or depth in the modern urban world, with its commercialisation and profane surfaces. But for Brown's city dwellers, as for Benjamin's flâneur, the city taunts or seduces with its flickering aura, and is simultaneously, I am arguing, the site of 'displacement of the religious into new forms of the sacred'.[12] Here is 'City', also from *50–50.*

City
A yearned-for somewhere
  adverb-physically
as lost as now
    gazing across
      the chunky valley
to a hill
  of quivering lights –

11. Brown, *50–50*, 71–72.
12. Paul Hegarty, 'Undelivered: the space/time of the sacred in Bataille and Benjamin', in *Economy and Society* 32/1 (2003): 114.

There is no
  destination –
just a place
  no site
not Olympic
    village site
not harbourside
    casino site
  nor section
    of expressway
      just east
of where
    coincidence
      has determined
        your residence
in a city
  you returned to
    to remember
      why you left–

Inventing
  nostalgia
    for elsewhere –

you'll live there
  in the future –[13]

The final dash—recalling another biting minimalist of the sacred, Emily Dickinson—is wonderful. Is it a linguistic lurch into the future, a beyond, it is postulating? Or another ironizing stroke of the computer key, signifying a no-place, no show? Is it a signifier of the *languaged nature* of that future? Here, place is emptied of its definitive meaning, emptied of sacredness, it might be argued, for here everything is negated—no destination, no site, not Olympic, not harbourside; and it is randomly circular, a place to which 'you returned to/to remember/why you left'; where 'coincidence' rhymes with 'residence'. But the city is also yearned for, a place that, because it *is* an invention, can be seen as *enabling* invention. And there is the flickering postmodern aura of meaning (possibility, substance): the quivering lights, the chunky valley, the shared story of vulnerability—yearn-

13. Brown, *50–50*, 28–29.

ing, gazing, memory—told only between the lines, and *in relation* to the city.

Sacred and profane places. One of the main projects of Georges Bataille, in 1930s and 40s France, as a leading member of the Parisian College of Sociology, was to invent Sacred Sociology.[14] He sought 'the profanation of the sacred'.[15]

His approach was 'to sites that predate modernity but persist within it . . . that could be characterised as (im)properly modern'.[16] As Bataille scholar Paul Hegarty writes, Bataille revealed

> . . . the transvaluation of sites valorized by Christianity in terms of holiness (the church, arguably the home . . .) or in terms of sin (the brothel, the bar, the woods) such that they are part of an economy of transgression, or of *an ever-mobile sacrifice* [my italics]. Only after such a shift in value, which is the removal of value (insofar as this fixes a phenomenon) can the move be made to bring back the religious sacred, this time as part of a Bataillean sacred, such that 'a brothel is my true church'.[17]

The premise here is that only in *the removal of value* can the sacred be opened towards. And it *is* a question of *experience* rather than fixed space, category, value or definition. As Hegarty describes it, sacred acts or places

> cannot permanently exist as sacred, but they can be brought . . . and this bringing requires time—a time not of progress, or even process, but of waiting, of non-occurrence because unrealizable—unliveable except in hindsight, except perhaps in anticipation of its not being liveable. But this space is far from abstract . . . [18]

This is not the sacred of the cathedral or mosque, bush or city. Nor is it the sacred of moral codes, nor of the legalism which often attends such codes. It is the experience of the individual and of a community (readership? peers?): what is yearned for, awaited, dreamed of, leaned towards, recognised as unpurchaseable in a linguistic or geographical or legal or material economy. It is the coming to realise that there is no destination (as Brown's metaphor writes it), even as you arrive at your latest port of call. But as

14. Hegarty, 'Undelivered', 101.
15. Hegarty, 'Undelivered', 109.
16. Hegarty, 'Undelivered', 109.
17. Bataille, cited in Hegarty, 'Undelivered', 109.
18. Hegarty, 'Undelivered', 105.

Hegarty argues, it is also far from abstract, this sacred. In Brown's 'City' the sacred and political are imbricated, in the comic refusal of all those alluring national and commercial and class-transcending promises—'no site/not Olympic/village site/not harbourside/ casino site/ nor section/ of expressway/ just east.' This sacred undermines fatuities and glittering prizes, just as Bataille's sacred understood the *bringing* of sacred experience away from fixed or institutional or codified versions of the religious, including most particularly for Bataille, European fascism.

In the anti-institutional and anti-colonising aspects of Bataille's sacred there are obviously synchronicities for artists working in contemporary, post-colonial Australia. But of course the context of the necessarily political and spiritual struggles against entrenched hierarchies and dogmas in early twentieth-century Europe is not the same context in which postmodern poets in the West are now working. What was at stake for Bataille and other anti-fascist artists was the need to disarm the mighty push towards political and religious centres, programmes that were yet again establishing themselves. For Brown and her peers, poets such as John Forbes, Ken Bolton and Laurie Duggan, there is a different, Australian starting point in relation to the making of meaning; and it seems almost a converse one in relation to any idea of the experience of meaning or sacredness: Brown's cynicism, satire, attractions and repulsions, seem built around an *absent* centre, something always already (in the poetry) lost in the tedious non-occurrences of contemporary (Australian) life. At times this absent centre seems to be what needs attacking, eradicating, repulsing. At other times it continues its function of holding out the possibility of meaning. In this latter context, Brown's poems are perpetually *beginning*:

> setting out,
> a scarlet flower
> behind an ear,
> into the wide
> world into
> banner-adorned cities
> faking
> permanent festivity[19]

or,

> leaving nature's

19. Brown, 'Anyworld', *Cordite*, at <www.cordite.org.au/archives/000488.html>. Accessed 7 December 2004.

barbarism (spider
in a glove) behind
me I enter my
paved city–
pocked concrete
& traffic carbon
sky's all
coppery night's
coming up

I follow
the man-in-the-dress
along a lane
littered
with litter
where
Carlo and Zanzi
have signed
the sub-station
roll-a-door–
more than a tag–
a declaration–
white strokes
wide brush[20]

Momentarily adorned as Romantic poet, 'a scarlet flower/behind an ear', the narrators of Brown's poems have to learn again and again that there is no return, that nature is barbaric, just as the city is, 'faking/permanent festivity', 'pocked concrete/& traffic carbon'. But her repulsions constantly, momentarily pivot into hope, a leaning towards, observing intimately 'my/ paved city'. This is not Blake's blasted London full of marked and desecrated citizens, nor the Armageddon of Eliot's *Wasteland.* Brown's poetry is less dramatic, more democratic, accepting, following without judgement 'the man-in-the-dress', observing the verve and particularity of Carlo and Zanzi's 'declaration', experiencing in the marks of 'her' city what she sees in herself—not the need for redemption arising out of some extraordinary fiat or mighty pronouncement, and possibly foreshadowing no redemption at all, but still a continuing need—in the citizens, in the poet—to declare, to sign, to transgress. Postmodern theologian Mark Taylor writes:

20. Brown, 'In Ultimo', *50–50* (Adelaide: Little Esther Books, 1997), 93–94.

> For Bataille, [the sacred is] the soiled, it's the dirty, it's the polluted, it's that which is ordinarily regarded as negative . . . Because he sees in that kind of hierarchical structure of high and low, extraordinary repression. And he's trying to release that—to cultivate, indeed solicit, the return of the repressed.[21]

At the end of the poem 'Anyworld' Brown declares:

> re mem ber Ba,
> Are-e Bam
> ancient city of sand
> and mud
> collapsing in an earthquake,
> the cultural heritage building
> slipping subsiding,
> consigning
> any record
> of the archaic ruin
> to dust
> *
> the memory
> is
> ruined
> *
> who can accept
> a given world,
> who can
> live in it?[22]

This essay has been reading in Brown's work an openness towards the littered, un-Romantic, pocked and transvestite city, 'my paved city'; to the transgressive, unaffiliated, anti-hierarchcical; to defilements, blankness and littleness. Brown's poetry places a finger on the pulse of small, everyday defilements, registering the mystery of abjection, of loss, and the unlocatableness of meaning. In 'Anyworld' all cities, including the human body, are sand and mud, collapsing. The final question of 'Anyworld'—'who can accept/a given world/who can/live in it'—is almost imponderable. The question strains with irony, the word 'accept' pulling in opposite

21. Taylor, 'Georges Bataille'.
22. Brown, 'Anyworld'.

directions: *not to accept* is to judge, condemn, repudiate, dismiss. But to judge what? In the context of this poem, to accept seems an act of complacency, a simple, total forgetting. But if the world is 'given', there is no direct mention here of a giver, divine or otherwise. Unless, in approaching that liminal place between acceptance and rage, living and refusing to live, the experience of the sacred emerges: a waiting, a non-occurrence, a mobility. Of course this poem's question is potentially moral and political, for one answer is—I will not accept, I will change the given world, as in Brown's poem 'At the Wall's' and its outrage over 'sarajevo srebrenica palestine/ rwanda kabul'. But a parallel, a certainly not mutually exclusive, response is to acknowledge the *sacred* dimension of the question, a sacredness experienced in this active play of possibility and impossibility. Mark Taylor writes of Bataille:

> . . . at the heart of the experience of the sacred is the conflict between attraction and repulsion. The sacred is never simply one or the other, it is at one and the same time attractive and repulsive. That's what lends it its power and horror. What happens in a lot of Christianity is that the positive and the negative get split and posited on two different realities—God and the Devil, whatever framework we're in.[23]

The rigor of Pam Brown's poetry lies in its very refusal to merely collapse into one or the other reality. There are no Gods or Devils, no unironic negatives and positives. Rather, I have been arguing that in Brown's poetry there are metaphorically rich experiences of a yearning, one which recognises language as the chief ally *and* enemy, the poetic site being not one of celebration *or* repulsion, but of both. The aura glimpsed fleetingly may well be only those flickering lights across the valley, but the poet makes them props in an experience '. . . of waiting, of non-occurrence . . . unrealizable—unliveable except in hindsight, except perhaps in anticipation of its (possibly) not being liveable'.[24] This is 'an ever mobile', languaged experience of sacredness encountered in the ordinary, faking, littered and flickering city.

23. Taylor, 'Georges Bataille'.
24. Hegarty, 'Undelivered', 105.

Works Cited

Bataille, Georges. *Inner Experience,* translated by Boldt, Leslie Anne (Albany: SUNY Press, 1988).

Brown, Pam. *Selected Poems 1971–1982* (Sydney: Redress/Wild&Woolley. 1984).

----*New & Selected Poems* (Sydney: Wild&Woolley, 1990).

----*This World. This Place* (Brisbane: University of Queensland Press, 1994).

----*Little Droppings* (Sydney: Never-Never Books, 1994).

----*50–50* (Adelaide: Little Esther Books, 1997).

----*Drifting Topoi* (Sydney: Vagabond Press, 2000).

----*Text Thing* (Adelaide: Little Esther Books, 2002).

----*Dear Deliria: New & Selected Poems* (UK/USA/Aus: Salt Publishing, 2003).

Brown, Pam, Bolton, Ken, and Duggan, Laurie, *Let's Get Lost* (Sydney: Vagabond Press, Stray Dog Editions, 2005).

Clément, Catherine, and Kristeva, Julie. *The Feminine And The Sacred*, translated by Todd, Jane Marie (New York: Columbia University Press, 2001).

Cordite. http://www.cordite.org.au/archives/000488.html. [Accessed Dec.7] 2004.

Hegarty, Paul. 'Undelivered: The Space/Time Of The Sacred In Bataille And Benjamin', in *Economy and Society* 32/1 (February 2003): 101–18.

Heimonet, Jean Michel. 'Bataille And Sartre: The Modernity Of Mysticism', in *Diacritics* 26/2 (Summer 1996): 59–73.

Henry, Brian. Review of *Dear Deliria: New And Selected Poems*, *Jacket* 23 (August 12, 2003). http://jacketmagazine.com/23/henry-brown.html.

Kristeva, Julia. *Powers of Horror: An Essay On Abjection*, translated by Roudiez, Leon S (New York: Columbia University Press, 1982).

McCann, Andrew. 'The Ethics Of Abjection: Patrick White's *Riders In The Chariot*', in *Australian Literary Studies* 18/2 (1997): 145–55.

----'Savage Metropolis: Animism, Aesthetics And The Pleasures Of A Vanished Race', in *Textual Practice* 17/2 (2003): 317–33.

Taylor, Mark. 'Georges Bataille', ABC Radio National, *Encounter*: 22/4/2001 Sunday 7.10pm. http:www.abc.net.au/rn/relig/enc/stories.

Chapter Nine

The Carnal Theologies of Nick Cave

Nick Cave is not a theologian. Nor does he claim to be one. What Cave's lyrics address, in multiple ways, however, is sacredness. While early twentieth century anthropologists and historians of religion such as Mircea Eliade tended to theorise 'the sacred' as 'the opposite of the profane',[1] Cave's sacred is deeply enmeshed in the human dimensions of flesh, erotics, and violence. The sacred—the holy, divine, hierophanic, epiphanic—and the profane do not stand apart in his work, but are in dynamic and sometimes conflicting conjunction, creating a sprawling, unsystematic and confrontational dialogue with divine forces which may or may not be 'there'. Institutional religion does not fare well in his lyrics, but nor is it ignored. What we find stamped across his songs, over and over, is the dark, lonely figure of a man caught up in desire for a divine source or balm.

Music journalist Roni Sarig writes evocatively that Cave's sixteenth album, *The Boatman's Call* (1997)

> sounds like Cave's attempt to poison his cake and eat it too. For a record so resolute in its denial of divinity, *The Boatman's Call's* obsession with religious themes and imagery might seem contradictory if they hadn't come from someone like Cave, who fancies himself a fallen angel searching for a ladder back to heaven. Where Gothic meets cathedral, there resides, for better or worse, our dark saint Nick.[2]

1. Mircea Eliade, *The Sacred and the Profane: The Nature of Religion*, translated by WR Trask (New York: Harcourt Brace Jovanovich, 1959), 10. For contemporary discussions on the conjunction of postmodernity and the sacred, including debates surrounding the relationship of the sacred and the profane, see Phillippa Berry and Andrew Wernick, editors, *Shadow of Spirit: Postmodernism and Religion* (New York and London, Routledge, 1992).
2. Roni Sarig. *Review of The Boatman's Call*, at <www.amazon.co.uk/Boatmans-Call-Nick-Cave/>. Accessed 28 August 2007.

Fallen angels and heavenly ladders notwithstanding, 'the poisoned, desirable cake' does indeed capture the ambivalent object of Cave's theology. But such ambivalence can be seen to arise not simply from the personality of Cave, self-styled 'fallen angel'. Rather, Cave's work is in a long line of gothic and Romantic writing which understands 'the beauty and the terror' of the created, carnal world. Gothic met cathedral long ago. In his most powerful songs a theology emerges which does not simply endure or oppose human violence, abjection and the flesh, but sees them as intimately entwined with any access to the sacred.

Many Cave song lyrics are tidal assaults on religious pieties and comforting clichés. Most of Cave's Birthday Party, Bad Seeds and solo song lyrics, written across twenty-five years, are available on the web. On a number of websites such as *All the Lyrics,* at the individual song level, there are advertisements for 'Christian Music' or 'SMS me bible scriptures: Daily scriptures txt to your mobile Bible SMS, five day free trial now!' There is also a link to 'Christ—The Hunger for Him, And the Adoring of Him. Everything he can do for Man and Woman', which leads you to a multilingual evangelical site headed 'The Missing Cross to Purity'.[3] As those Christian website advertisers recognise, there are crossovers here. Cave may not— and surely could not—attract the religious fundamentalists, but his many addresses to God, the pleas for justice in this world and the next, and the desire to invoke and embrace a God who so often transmutes into divine absence are what constitute Cave's arena of the sacred. What might be Cave's sacred: part prophetic Jesus, part Father in the Christian tradition, part old testament force of retribution, part metonym for human love and sexual energy, part violent power with unknown capabilities, part absence, part extension of the Cave ego. Is there a system to Cave's sacred? (And does that matter?) That is, can we discern in the spectrum of the songwriter's attention to the sacred anything like recurring chords, not to say a manifesto or theology? Or does 'God' in the many Cave manifestations of sacredness amount to a convenient—or monstrous—hole into which the songwriter pours his own psychic imaginings?

I will argue, through a reading of the lyrics, that what we have in Cave's work amounts to an idiosyncratic but also embracingly contemporary theology of the fleshed or carnal sacred, given the darkly erotic and violent contexts in which Cave's visions of sacredness unfold so often. Take

3. *All the Lyrics*, at <www.allthelyrics.com>. Accessed 10 August 2007.

for example the song 'Brompton Oratory'.[4] The setting for this lyric is the nineteenth century baroque and Italianate Oratory of St Philip Neri, a Roman Catholic repository of excessive aesthetics, including the twelve stone apostles in the Nave referred to in the second stanza, carved in 1680 for the Cathedral in Siena. Into this 'great shadowed vault' the melancholic, defiant lover, a recurrent Cave figure, trails his grief. He has lost love, it seems, and is a seeker of divine comfort while simultaneously doubting the existence—or availability to humanity—of such a divine force:

> Up those stone steps I climb
> Hail this joyful day's return
> Into its great shadowed vault I go
> Hail the Pentecostal morn
> The reading is from Luke 24
> Where Christ returns to his loved ones
> I look at the stone apostles
> Think that it's alright for some
> And I wish that I was made of stone
> So that I would not have to see
> A beauty impossible to define
> A beauty impossible to believe
> A beauty impossible to endure
> The blood imparted in little sips
> The smell of you still on my hands
> As I bring the cup up to my lips

In the brooding words, set in odd juxtaposition to the quietly buoyant, syncopated rhythm, many contradictions open out: the morn is Pentecostal for the speaker, a joyful return, but he wishes he was made of stone in order not to feel so much. The day's reading in the mass is *Luke* 24, which contains the central Christian narrative of transcendence, the resurrection of Christ; but the song merely describes the passage as narrating 'Christ's return to his loved ones', a wonderful use of Cave understatement. But the core tension of the song, reflected in these many smaller tensions, is that of the lover's condition, between flesh and spirit: 'the smell of you still on my hands/ As I bring the cup up to my lips'. It remains uncertain the extent to which the loss he is lamenting is carnal, and in what ways his melancholic state—'Forlorn and exhausted, baby/ By the absence of

4. Nick Cave, 'Brompton Oratory', *The Boatman's Call* (Reprise / Wea, 1997).

you'—opens out into a spiritual hunger in the absence of the divine, a state evident in the singer's prayer, or wish, that he might be

> made of stone,
> So that I would not have to see
> A beauty impossible to define,
> A beauty impossible to believe,
>
> A beauty impossible to endure,
> The blood imparted in little sips.

The beauty here can refer equally to the fleshed lover and to a divine impossibility—conjoined here in a secular prayer—to be turned to stone like the twelve apostles who look down from their unfeeling perches at suffering men and women.

Rhythmically, the final stanza's stress draws out the word 'Aaab-sence', making it palpable; but we have also just heard in sensuous, immediate terms of the woman's bodily presence for him, at the very point of the mass when the divine presence is invoked. In this way the experience of the ritual—of worship and communion—is both healing and estranging, for this is a theology which emerges from earthy, fleshed desires: the communion wine is described directly and simply as 'the blood' and it mingles immediately with 'The smell of you still on my hands'. The contradiction—some might say blasphemy[5]—embraced in these opposites being brought into relation, also fuels the penultimate stanza's cry:

> No God up in the sky,
> No devil beneath the sea,
> Could do the job that you did, baby,
> Of bringing me to my knees.

Sexual and religious submission conjoin here. This invoking of the very sexual, bodily forces, which traditionally should be displaced in order to worship a transcendent god, telescope together the erotic and the divine.

---

5. Blasphemy according to the Merriam-Webster dictionary has three main stems: 1) the act of insulting or showing contempt or lack of reverence for God. 2) the act of claiming the attributes of deity. 3) irreverence toward something considered sacred or inviolable. While this essay does not attribute blasphemy to Cave's writing, it is possible to see how some would read his equation of human love with the divine as blasphemous according to the second attribute, let alone his questioning of violence as implicated in, if not related to the divine.

Further, there is a fusing of sexual and divine love, of the powers of the loved woman with those of god and devil, which register the essence of Cave's sacred vision: the inescapable, incarnate force of the divine.[6] The loved woman is just as absent as God or devil, but the presence of all meet in the suppliant brought to his knees. The language of the song, together with its syncopated, insistent, forward tilting rhythm, invoke a love which is in mourning at the bodily absence of its loved object, but simultaneously registers the body and its senses as the real paths to the spirit. It is one example of Cave's many representations of melancholia as enabling, the site of fusion between body and spirit.

So, 'Brompton Oratory' entangles the sacred with the abject—the blood, the tears, the pain, the sacrifice in human to human and human to divine relations. The murdered or tortured body, brought to its knees, is a recurrent motif for Cave. His lyrics, and the motivating force of his ongoing artistic practice, are permeated with a discourse which parallels Julia Kristeva's theory of abjection, and in particular its effects in the evolution of traditional religions into *artistic* forms of sacredness:

> The various means of *purifying* the abject—the various catharses—make up the history of religions, and end up with that catharsis par excellence called art, both on the far and near side of religion. Seen from that standpoint, the artistic experience, which is rooted in the abject it utters and by the same token purifies, appears as the essential component of religiosity. That is perhaps why it is destined to survive the collapse of the historical forms of religions.[7]

This 'religiosity' is apparent in Cave's enduringly melancholic encounters with the abject limits of the human—the violence done to the corpse, the entanglement of innocence with darkly erotic drives. Kristeva outlines here the connections of art as a practice in its relationship to abjection and

6. Incarnational theology covers a broad spectrum of beliefs. Christian incarnationalism is discussed by Jerry H Gill, 'Faith in Learning: Integrative Education and Incarnational Theology', in *Christian Century* (17 October 1979): 1009: 'Human existence is embodied existence, and God's involvement and interaction with us have come in this mode. In the Judeo-Christian tradition the body is basic and good, in contrast to the dualism of classical Greek philosophy . . . By indwelling (not just 'borrowing') a body, God made a statement about the nature and worth of human existence—and about divine character as well. Moreover, the Christian hope is for a resurrected body, as well as a new heaven and earth, not for the immortality of a disembodied soul'.
7. Julia Kristeva, 'Approaching Abjection', in *Powers of Horror: An Essay on Abjection*, translated by Leon S Roudiez (New York and London, 1982), 1–31; 17.

the sacred. The multiple artistic acts of representing and engaging with the abject—cartharsis, self-abasement, guilt, blood sacrifice, the body of the other, railing against the cruelties of fate or the divine—are Cave's par excellence; consider, for example, 'Idiot Prayer' as the murderer envisages his victim/lover, 'Your face comes to me from the depths, dear/ Your silent mouth mouths, 'Yes', dear/ Dark red and big with blood' (*Boatman's Call,* 1997). We see an abject approach too in the threat issued to stained sinners: 'you'll scrub and you'll scrub/ But the trouble is, bud/ The blood it won't wash off/ No, it won't come off! ('City of Refuge', *Tender Prey*, 1988); or the grim lament of 'Darker by the Day', with its condemned man finding in the scriptures 'a woolly lamb dozing in an issue of blood/ And a gilled Jesus shivering on a fisherman's hook' (*No More Shall We Part* 2001).[8]

The abject is in part what draws out a fascination with those liminal spaces where the body melts into fluid, or waste, where it encounters 'the other' to its own supposed solidity, in death, or other kinds of transmogrification. The album *The Boatman's Call* introduces us to the mythical gothic Boatman suggestive of that important liminal figure, Charon, controller of the passenger list for that final journey across the river Styx to the Underworld. Charon has the power to ban the dead from his boat, condemning them to haunt the riverbanks for centuries. It is a highly evocative album title, pointing to Cave's own prophetic, playful and serious sense of vocation in his songwriting. His songs are bridges between earthly and sacred places, or more aptly, they are transitory and often teetering structures pushing out beyond the limits of sense, order and proper knowledge.

'Into my Arms' from *The Boatman's Call,* perhaps Cave's commercially best-known song, gives us the same unbeliever hovering between belief and unbelief. While he cannot accept the proposition of 'an interventionist god', he addresses his own doubt with the repeated structure: I can't believe, but if I did I would kneel . . .

> I don't believe in an interventionist God,
> But I know, darling, that you do.
> But if I did I would kneel down and ask Him
> Not to intervene when it came to you

8. Nick Cave, *Tender Prey* (Mute USA, 1988); *The Boatman's Call* (Reprise/Wea, 1997); *No More Shall We Part* (Reprise/Wea, 2001).

> Not to touch a hair on your head
> To leave you as you are
> And if He felt He had to direct you
> Then direct you into my arms

There is a gentle, high-serious humour at play in the repeated structure, a doubter's dialogue with his (hypothetically) believing self. The loved one is given god-like presence, is to be worshipped, surrounded by angels; but so too is the singer, who proceeds to give his own directions to this non-existent god: not to intervene, not to touch a hair on your head, to leave you as you are. In the final stanza the lover does become a believer 'in love', 'in some kind of path'. His request—

> keep your candles burning
> Make a journey bright and pure
> That she'll keep returning
> Always and evermore
>
> Into my arms, O Lord

—seems at first a request to the lover, but it becomes a prayer, an address to a Lord who just might have the power to intervene, to broaden the reach and intensity of the love experienced, to enable the lovers to 'walk, like Christ, in grace and love'.

The middle stanza of 'Into my arms' teases and is seductive in its imagined merging of the divine and the human. The lover reveals himself and his love as humanly vulnerable to harm and time, and in need of divine intervention, with the song's chorus—'into my arms, O Lord'—reiterating an image of both sexual union and the protective figure of the old testament, interventionist God: 'The eternal God is your refuge, and underneath are the everlasting arms'.[9]

Many of the lyrics on *The Boatman's Call* hold this tension between doubt and belief, with the anthemic 'There is a Kingdom' declaring belief more fulsomely than most:

> There is a kingdom
> There is a king
> And he lives without
> And he lives within

9. Deuteronomy 33:27.

> There is a kingdom
> There is a king
> There is a king
> And he is everything

The voice and the swelling hymn-like repetitions are prophetic, pointing to an incarnate king, within and without, encompassing 'everything'. The song draws on a thoroughgoing kind of incarnationalism. Yet within this song, and more overtly in earlier songs such as 'Swing Low', 'The Mercy Seat', and 'O My Lord', there is also a violence that the sacred does not simply oppose, but with which it seems to be enmeshed. The first stanza of 'There is a kingdom' is in a voice whose source is hard to pin down:

> Just like a bird that sings up the sun
> In a dawn so very dark
> Such is my faith for you
> Such is my faith
> And all the world's darkness can't swallow up
> A single spark
> Such is my love for you
> Such is my love

The voice is God-like, pronouncing with unquenchable faith that not 'a single spark' of light will be swallowed up by the world's darkness. The locution is odd—'such is my faith for you'. Is it a creator God speaking with faith in his creation? Is it a Christ figure, bearing the faith 'for' all humanity? At one level, the imagination is Manichean[10] here, creating a world split between light and darkness: 'the starry heavens above me', 'this mist of tears' surrounding. However, there is equally, and even contradictorily, an incarnational understanding at work too, a desire which insists on the all-encompassing, immanent and palpable divine kingdom, already present, if only we could see it 'in this sweet day'.

'There is a Kingdom' only indirectly suggests a world of sacred warfare which might be characterised as 'Old Testament', except that it is also characteristic of so-called Christian fundamentalist notions of 'spiritual

10. Manicheanism is both a religion, which arose in Persia in the third century AD, and a more general term denoting a polarisation or split between distinct opposites, such as good and evil, body and spirit. For a contemporary scholarly account of Manicheanism and its relationship to Christian theology through the theology of Augustine, see J Kevin Coyle, *The Manichean Debate* (New York, 2007).

warfare' as well. The second part of the biblical text from Deuteronomy quoted previously—'The eternal God is your refuge, and underneath are the everlasting arms'—states: 'He will thrust out the enemy from before you, and will say, 'Destroy!' 'There is a Kingdom' invokes the human desire for such a place beyond the dark and unjust world of tears. The register of many Cave songs is apocalyptically Manichean and retributive, however, intrigued by divine and human eschatological scenarios.

For example, if we move back in history to Cave's 1988 album *Tender Prey* we find songs such as 'Mercy', which is not particularly about mercy, but about warfare between evil forces and a figure who appears to be John the Baptist, standing in water in 'the middle month of winter', deserted by his followers:

> Thrown into a dungeon
> Bread and water was my portion
> Faith—my only weapon
> To rest the devil's legion
> The speak-hole would slide open
> A viper's voice would plead
> Thick with innuendo
> Syphilis and Greed
> And she cried 'Mercy'

The voice of the viper through the speak-hole mockingly mouthing the words of repentance—'thick with innuendo/ Syphilis and Greed'—represents all the worldly evils ranged against the saint; the solitary martyr against 'the devil's legion'. The Baptist is touchingly vulnerable, crying out for mercy, wondering if his cousin who is performing miracles elsewhere will find him. If we know the story we know it won't happen, he will not receive mercy, at least in this world. The vision of the moon, 'turned toward me/ Like a platter made of gold' reminds us about where he is heading.

'City of Refuge' from the same album also separates the sheep from the goats in Manichean terms:

> You better run, you better run
> You better run to the City of Refuge.
> You stand before your maker
> In a state of shame,
> Because your robes are covered in mud
> While you kneel at the feet

Of a woman of the street
The gutters will run with blood
They will run with blood!

This is apocalyptic theology with its vision of the last days. It is a world riven into two parts, with refuge for the believer and gutters running with blood and shame for the rest in those days 'of madness/ My brother, my sister / When you're dragged toward the Hell-mouth'. This kind of religious discourse would be at home in those old-time evangelists' tents in the American South. As in *The Ass saw the Angel* we can see here Cave's fascination with images of heaven and hell, of apocalyptic climax. Cave's fascination with such contexts and the promise they seem to offer of unequivocal judgement, might be read as a part of his ongoing desire for justice and its manifest absence in human affairs. This is a path fundamentalists—political and religious—often take, but Cave is far from fundamentalist in the uses to which he puts such desire for justice.

For example, Cave's film script and score for *The Proposition*[11] are steeped in images of frontier violence, revenge and retribution; yet the narrative does not provide a polarising or simplistic solution. Captain Stanley, played with vulnerable physicality by actor Ray Winstone, begins by seeing himself in stark terms as 'an agent of civilisation' come to dispatch the brutish Burns brothers, particularly the gang's charismatic and violent leader Arthur. In setting out his proposition to younger brother Charlie, a plan to capture the maniacal Arthur, Stanley says:

> He is out there, where no man should be. While in town, God fearing Christians whisper his name. But no one, Charlie, no one talks about what he did at the Hopkins' homestead. Though you and I, and little Mikey here, we know what happened there . . . and we all know who was responsible for the atrocity . . . [12]

Here we have a retrospective vision of colonial violence and brutality, a twenty-first century version of a world which emerges partly from the genre of the Western, with its good guy/ bad guy frontier heroics, but imbued with a violent metaphysical register too. Arthur's violence is beyond humanity, beyond what the 'God fearing Christians' of the town can speak

11. Nick Cave, *The Proposition*, filmscript (Independent film, director John Hillcoat, 2005). http://www.rouge.com.au/7/cave.html.
12. Nick Cave, *The Proposition*, filmscript (Independent film, director John Hillcoat, 2005). http://www.rouge.com.au/7/cave.html.

aloud. The savagery seems to be even more heinous because the killing of the Hopkins family was carried out by 'its own kind', by white men, Irish men, and not 'even' by the blacks. Again, Stanley stands up to the evil he sees embodied in Burns:

> I know where Arthur Burns is. It is a bad place. The blacks will not go there. Not even the black trackers . . . I suppose, in time the bounty hunters will get him. But I have other plans. I aim to bring him down. I aim to show that he is a man like any other. I aim to hurt him. Well I've thought long and hard about that.[13]

However, while Stanley's speech begins in fundamentalist terms, it inadvertently acknowledges the humanity of his quarry ('a man like any other'), and his own desire for violence ('I aim to hurt him'). The twist that Cave performs in *The Proposition* is in allowing us to glimpse the contradictory charisma of Arthur, a man who can poetically grasp the beauty of the land he rides through, as well as commit atrocious acts of violence. This doubleness of character is a typical Cave vision, one that sometimes calls on a response of forgiveness (we are all capable of being an ass *and* an angel) and sometimes on retribution. Equally, Stanley comes to realise the naiveté, if not arrogance, of his own policing version of reality in a place far from the halls of British justice. One overarching realization offered by *The Proposition* is of the raw physicality, even the brutishness of all human attempts at justice, and the scapegoating and bloodletting that our fallenness necessarily entails.

French theorist of religions René Girard theorises the historical ties between art, violence and the sacred. In his highly influential work he focuses on the scapegoat, the figure that takes the full force of ancient societal warring, but a figure that also enables the primitive urge towards violence to be repressed in 'modern' societies. Girard's historical and anthropological studies of religions reveal two significant and counterpointed aspects of violence, scapegoating and bloodletting, expressed powerfully in his accounts of blood, that abject medium, symbol of both cleansing and violence:

13. Nick Cave, *The Proposition*, filmscript (Independent film, director John Hillcoat, 2005). http://www.rouge.com.au/7/cave.html.

> Only blood itself, blood whose purity has been guaranteed by the performance of appropriate rites—the blood in short, of sacrificial victims—can accomplish this feat . . .
> The properties of blood, for example, vividly illustrate the entire operation of violence . . . Blood that dries on the victim soon looses its viscous quality and becomes first a dark sore, then a roughened scab. Blood that is allowed to congeal on its victim is the impure product of violence, illness or death. In contrast to this contaminated substance is the fresh blood of newly slaughtered victims, crimson and free flowing.[14]

On Cave's album *Murder Ballads*[15] (sometimes referred to as Cave's 'joke' album for its often camp renditions of old crime narratives) the grim song of the lonely traveller in 'Song of Joy' takes the notion of sacrifice, and of the ancient human propensity for violence and grief, to its intimate source in the bosom of the family and sexual love. The bloodletting in 'Song of Joy' is well described by Girard's first notion of impure and unredeeming blood. The narrator of the song appears as a stranger at the door of a house one frozen night asking for mercy and a place to say. He proceeds, uninvited, to tell the tale of his wife Joy, their three little girls, and the slow spiral of their life together into horror and death. Joy quickly turns from a 'sweet and happy thing', to a melancholic creature with haunted eyes, 'As if she saw into the heart of her final blood-soaked night/ Those lunatic eyes, that hungry kitchen knife'. On her final night while the husband was away visiting a sick friend his wife is

> bound with electrical tape,
> In her mouth a gag.
> She'd been stabbed repeatedly
> And stuffed into a sleeping bag.
> In their very cots my girls were robbed of their lives
> Method of murder much the same as my wife's
> Method of murder much the same as my wife's

As listeners we are asked simultaneously to sympathise with the poor husband, but also to be suspicious. The storyteller husband has witnessed carnal mayhem, but like that earlier metaphysical traveller the Ancient

14. René Girard, *Violence and the Sacred*, translated by Patrick Gregory (Baltimore: Johns Hopkins University Press, 1977), 36–37.
15. Nick Cave, *Murder Ballads* (Reprise/Wea, 1996).

Mariner he is strangely obsessive and intruding, marked by the blood of his family, not clean:

> I drift from land to land.
> I am upon your step and you are a family man.
> Outside the vultures wheel,
> The wolves howl, the serpents hiss.
> And to extend this small favour, friend,
> Would be the sum of earthly bliss.
> Do you reckon me a friend?

The narrator here is one of Cave's losers in love, but with a markedly violent twist. We have to ask: Is he murderer *as well as* victim? The graffiti left by the murderer is by

> John Milton on the walls in the victim's blood.
> The police are investigating at tremendous cost.
> In my house he wrote 'his red right hand.'

Cave places us momentarily in *Paradise Lost* where all are both victims and perpetrators, fallen creatures. So many of Cave's lovers are murderers, so many are the ones sinned against. Many are both. This vision of the double nature of humans haunts Cave's theology, and perhaps is responsible for the often passive aggression (melancholic defiance?) of his lovers. Girard's theory of violence within the sacred has another theoretical turn, though, and moves away from the historical and evolving sense of ritual sacrifice and bloodletting towards a Christian understanding of the relationship between violence, sacredness and love:

> The Logos of love puts up no resistance; it always allows itself to be expelled by the Logos of violence. But its expulsion is revealed in a more and more obvious fashion, and by the same process the Logos of violence is revealed as what can only exist by expelling the true Logos and feeding upon it in one way or another.[16]

This is not exactly the feel of 'Song of Joy', however. It is more appropriate perhaps as the back story to 'Brompton Oratory'. Girard's theory here is full of images from *Paradise Lost*: Logos against Logos; violence, which

16. René Girard, *Things Hidden Since the Foundation of the World*, translated by Stephen Bann (London: Athlone, 1987), 274.

leads to expulsion from the garden, met by the long processes of redemption through a sacrificial Logos of love. But Milton, like Girard and Cave, also enshrines a less polarised figure of Lucifer, if we are to believe William Blake's description of Milton as 'of the Devil's party without knowing it'.[17] Cave, though, is a shifty and much less consistent—or less dogmatic—theologian than Milton or Blake. This very shiftiness, the constantly hungry imagination of Cave, is perhaps his salvation. Nowhere does he claim definitive positions on religion or the divine, but everywhere he is measuring the capacity of his words to stretch towards the sacred.

Cave's fleshed sacred is characterised by sexual energy (or its loss), as much as by violence. It often takes on prophetic resonances, but nowhere does it claim the mantle of religion. In her 1999 essay on performance art and the escalating use of blood and violence, critic Dawn Perlmutter writes:

> artists are increasingly using blood and violence in art and audiences are attending. This art can be referred to as 'postmodern mortification' because it represents a spiritual attempt by artists to dismantle personal and societal boundaries through physical sacrifice as a ritual form of purification. Although . . . this fails as religious ritual, it is a ritual process nonetheless. What will define the progress of this genre is not so much the artists as the audience. If audience participation begins to take place, participation being defined as religious interaction and communal transformation, performance art will no longer be positioned in the category of the aesthetic but will be designated by society as a new religious movement.[18]

While Cave is not a performance artist per se, he does *perform* his theology; and his work does ask for more response from an audience than swaying to the beat. It is, in line with Perlmutter's descriptions of performance art and its reach, arguably too playful and self-mocking to fall into the category of 'a new religious movement'. Cave's art, nevertheless, does have designs upon its audiences. It does call out prophetically, pointing towards human sexuality, love, desire to worship, dying, grief and bodiliness as processes encompassed by the sacred. On the early album *Tender Prey*, 'The Mercy Seat' is a strange, gothic and performative narrative, a

17. William Blake, *The Marriage of Heaven and Hell* (London: Dent, 1927 [1793]), 373.
18. Dawn Perlmutter, 'The Sacrificial Aesthetic: Blood Rituals from Art to Murder', in *Anthropoetics* 5/2 (1999–2000): 11.

dialogue half sung, half spoken, which warps together human retributive justice and a different, hoped for 'beyond' of death. It is a *performance* in that the speaker is constructing and deconstructing the self before our eyes in a macabre dance of self-exposure:

> Like my good hand I
> Tatooed e.v.i.l. across its brother's fist
> That filthy five! They did nothing to challenge or resist.
>
> In heaven his throne is made of gold
> The ark of his testament is stowed
> A throne from which I'm told
> All history does unfold.
> Down here it's made of wood and wire
> And my body is on fire
> And god is never far away.
> Into the mercy seat I climb
> My head is shaved, my head is wired
> And like a moth that tries
> To enter the bright eye
> I go shuffling out of life
> Just to hide in death awhile
> And anyway I never lied.

Very much in the spirit of the film *Dead Man Walking*[19] which came out two years after *Tender Prey*, this song enacts the last moments of a man who has obviously been violent, his good hand not knowing what his evil hand did. The song charts the progress to the mercy seat; it also charts the progress from denial of his own actions, to an acknowledgement that he has lied, that he is not innocent. The sacred dimension of the song comes not in the personal biography being narrated but in the way mercy becomes palpable. There are many images offered for this 'place' of mercy, the electric chair being the starkest and most ironic: heaven's golden throne, the bright eye of god, death as rest. It is in the condemned man's desires, however, his longing for a place beyond this world's 'measuring of truth', that the place of mercy can be located. While there is a grim bravado in his acceptance of his fate, there is also forgiveness of himself, a 'nearly wholly innocent' man. The narrative traces his admission of his crimes, but underneath this a different notion of mercy or grace operates,

19. *Dead Man Walking* (Gramercy Films, director Tim Robbins, 1995).

one which does not depend on his 'works'—his guilt or innocence—but on his acknowledgement of his own body, his life as always both good and evil:

> My kill-hand is called e.v.i.l.
> Wears a wedding band that's g.o.o.d.
> `tis a long-suffering shackle
> Collaring all that rebel blood.

This is not the performative centre of the song, but it is the sacred centre. In fact in some ears it may sound like special pleading or self-justifying, but this moment, which understands criminality not just as individual pathology, nor as spectacle, but as the universal human condition, is a theologically rich insight. Death is understood and embraced within this insight as both frightening and welcoming. It becomes the place of solace, or at least the portal into another place.

Further, the song perplexingly conjoins images of the electric chair—symbol of retributive law, punishment, proof, sin, human justice—with the mercy seat of a saviour who might also have died in bodily form 'like some ragged stranger'. The implications of this conjunction are not clear-cut, of course. Is the grisly chair of wires and smoke and burning an instrument of divine justice, or is it the antithesis of any merciful God:

> In heaven his throne is made of gold,
> The ark of his testament is stowed,
> A throne from which I'm told
> All history does unfold.
> Down here it's made of wood and wire
> And my body is on fire
> And god is never far away.

Does this comparison of sacred and profane realms of justice draw the two spheres together, underlining their collusion, or does it imagine their vast difference? The question is left open in true Cave style, leaving a perplexing entanglement of horror at the violent corporeality of human justice. There is a complicating sense of *necessary* bloodletting, and a hope for a different world no longer having to judge 'All things either good or ungood', a realm of grace. The compulsive, whipping rhythms of the song create an urgency, almost panic, in the expressed need for such a place.

It is arguably in the less resolved, more ambiguous songs like 'Mercy Seat', and in his later work such as the 2001 album *No More Shall We Meet,* that we find Cave's most haunting theology, where divine and human intermingle, or impinge on each other in dialogic and disturbing ways. The world inhabited by the lovers in 'Gates of the Garden' (*No More Shall We Meet*) is one that is haunted, ancient and dying:

> Beneath the creeping shadow of the tower
> The bell from St. Edmunds informs me of the hour.
> I turn to find you waiting there for me,
> In sunlight and I see the way that you breathe,
> Alive and leaning on the gates of the garden,
> Alive and leaning on the gates of the garden,
> All alive and leaning on the gates of the garden.
> Leave these ancient places to the angels,
> Let the saints attend to their keeping of their cathedrals,
> And leave the dead beneath the ground so cold,
> For God is in this hand that I hold,
> As we open up the gates.
> As we open up the gates,
> We open up the gates of the garden.
> Won't you meet me at the gates,
> Won't you meet me at the gates,
> Won't you meet me at the gates
> To the garden.

The temporal world, so poignantly evoked in Cave's world weary, slow, almost spoken presentation on 'The Gates of the Garden', is one of abjection and death, populated by 'Fugitive fathers, sickly infants, decent mothers/ Runaways and suicidal lovers'. However, the imaginative work of the song enacts a return to 'the garden' and to an originary moment where human, sexual, breathing love provides a path of return: 'For God is in this hand I hold'. While the song is a Romantic plea to the lover—'Won't you meet me at the gates'—there seems to be a confidence that the desire will be met. She is there, 'alive and leaning on the gates to the garden'.

In the sadder, abject 'Hallelujah' from the same album, the coddled and timid narrator has lost the thread of his desire and his art: 'My typewriter had turned mute as a tomb/ And my piano crouched in the corner of my room/ With all its teeth bared'. While his nurse, who feeds and governs him, is away he momentarily attempts a journey; while his pyjamas are clinging to him 'like a shroud' he nevertheless begins to sing 'hallelujah', for

There rose before me a little house
With all hope and dreams kept within.
A woman's voice close to my ear
Said, 'Why don't you come in here?'
'You looked soaked to the skin'
Soaked to the skin, soaked to the skin,
soaked to the skin.
Hallelujah Hallelujah
Hallelujah Hallelujah.
I turned to the woman and the woman was young.
I extended a hearty salutation,
But I knew if my nurse had been here
She would never in a thousand years
Permit me to accept that invitation.

Cave lays before us his little parable of desire and hope pitted against human fear and containment. The song contemplates the wisdom of Blake's 'Bring me my Bow of burning gold:/ Bring me my Arrows of desire',[20] but the narrator resigns from his journey, turning away from reckless passion. Here, as so often in Cave, desire and imagination are erotically *and* compassionately charged, emerging from 'A woman's voice close to my ear', free from the prohibitions of the nurse and her salvation of cocoa and medication. The freedom, youth, and erotic drive on that 'first day of May' are pitched against the stern practicality of the nay-sayers and the narrator's own human timidity. Dried up imagination and pain are met by a reckless 'Hallelujah'. In fact, each chorus of 'Hallelujah' emerges directly from the moments of abjection, as if produced from those moments, but also in order to combat them. However, the struggle can not be sustained, the song ending in a funereal chorus—perhaps the twenty pretty girls who will carry his twenty buckets of tears, as he turns away from the beckoning of his desires.

Art and the imagination are the preeminent tools in Cave's evocations of the sacred. As with Blake, it is the shrivelling censors and prohibitors who shrink the image of God. In the song 'God is in the House', a hymn-like parody of American fundamentalist imagination sung by Cave with a flickering Southern drawl, the singer is a small-town nay-sayer who wants to tidy up the world of its crime and violence and alterity:

20. William Blake, 'Milton: And Did Those Feet in Ancient Times' (poem, 1804) in *The Portable Blake*, edited by Alfred Kazin (New York: The Viking Press, 1971), 11.

For God is in the house
God is in the house
God is in the house
And no one's left in doubt
God is in the house
Homos roaming the streets in packs
Queer bashers with tyre-jacks
Lesbian counter-attacks
That stuff is for the big cities
Our town is very pretty
We have a pretty little square
We have a woman for a mayor
Our policy is firm but fair
Now that God is in the house
God is in the house
God is in the house
Any day now He'll come out
God is in the house
Well-meaning little therapists
Goose-stepping twelve-stepping Teetotalitarianists
The tipsy, the reeling and the drop down pissed
We got no time for that stuff here
Zero crime and no fear
And we've bred all our kittens white
So that you can see them in the night
And at night we're on our knees
As quiet as a mouse
Since the word got out
From the North down to the South
For no-one's left in doubt
There's no fear about
If we all hold hands and very quietly shout
Hallelujah
God is in the house
God is in the house
Oh I wish He would come out
God is in the house

As with so many Cave songs, the lyrics together with his *performance* of the parody lead us in several directions. The small-town religious folk are satirised, their imagination so tiny and legalistic that they shrink to the size of mice, timidly singing up a god of zero crime, white kittens, no fear, no doubt. In fact they have created a toy god, just as rigid and tiny as they are. This seems to be the purport of the words. But the performance, with its sweet, slow rhythms, with their hint of a choir on the chorus, is moving. What is it we are moved by? It seems that at the point of highest political mockery there is pity and understanding even for the timid believers who act out of fear of an abject, violent world. All those 'well-meaning little therapists/goose-stepping twelve-stepping Teetotalitarianists' are, like Cave, dreaming of a better world. Their failure, it seems, is that they will not let God out of the house. Boxed-in, tamed, homogenised and purified, their god presides over a quaking congregation. Outside—'Homos roaming the streets in packs/ Queer bashers with tyre-jacks/ Lesbian counter-attacks'—is no place for their god.

But that very world is the one Cave inhabits. That world of abjection and violence, of elusive erotic possibilities, of loved and degraded flesh—'The tipsy, the reeling and the drop down pissed'—bodies forth the sacred. Dreaming of another place of mercy and justice beyond the fleshed world sometimes leads Cave to separate the sacred from the profane. However, his complex poetic theology also reaches for a vision of sacred and profane, flesh and spirit, as already everywhere in this world. As we saw in 'There is a Kingdom', and in so many of his lyrics, Cave is an artist impelled equally by darkness and light: 'Just like a bird that sings up the sun/ In a dawn so very dark' ('There is a Kingdom').

It is *artists* who are capable of not only singing up the sun, but doing it rapt in the mantle of darkness. Redemption is imagined by Cave, but rarely without the accompanying shadows of uncertainty. However, in the blackness of Cave's imagined world—its violence and bloodletting, its despised and yearning denizens, its often tragic eroticism—his characters are not 'swallowed up', finally. They emerge—stagger forward, wander sadly to your door, insist on telling you their tale of loss or threat, seduce you with their longing—clothed in both flesh and spirit.

Works Cited

All the Lyrics (2007) http://www.allthelyrics.com) Accessed Aug. 17.

Berry, Phillippa and Wernick, Andrew editors. *Shadow Of Spirit: Postmodernismand Religion* (London and New York: Routledge, 1992).

Blake, William (1793/1927). *The Marriage of Heaven and Hell* (London: Dent, 1793/1927).

----'Milton: And Did Those Feet In Ancient Times' (poem, 1804) in *The Portable Blake*, edited by Kazin, Alfred (New York: The Viking Press, 1804/1971.

Cave, Nick. *No More Shall We Part* (album) (London: Reprise/Wea, 2001).

----'Introduction to *Mark*', *The Pocket Canons Bible Series* (London: Canongate Books, 1991).

----'Brompton Oratory' (song), *The Boatman's Call* (London: Reprise / Wea, 1997).

---- *Murder Ballads* (album) (London: Reprise/Wea, 1996).

----*Tender Prey* (album), (Belgium: Mute U.SA, 1988).

Coyle, J Kevin. *The Manichean Debate* (New York: New City Press, 2007).

Eliade, Mircea. *The Sacred And The Profane: The Nature of Religion*, translated by Trask, WR (Paris: Harvest/HBJ Publishers, 1957).

Gill, Jerry H. 'Faith In Learning: Integrative Education And Incarnational Theology', in *Christian Century* (17 October 1979): 1009–1018.

Girard, René. *Violence And The* Sacred, translated by Gregory, Patrick (Baltimore: The Johns Hopkins University Press, 1972/1979).

----*Things Hidden Since The Foundation Of The World*, translated by Bann, Stephen (Stanford: Stanford University Press, 1987).

Haze, Lola. Review of *The Ass Saw The Angel*. http://www.amazon.com/Ass-saw-Angel-Nick-Cave/ Accessed 15 August 2007.

Hillcoat, John, director. *The Proposition* (Independent film, 2005). Filmscript and original score, Nick Cave. Extracts from Nick Cave's shooting script for

The Proposition. Rouge press © autonomous and UK Film Council, 2001. http://www.rouge.com.au/7/cave.html.

Kristeva, Julia. *Powers of Horror: An Essay On Abjection*, translated by Roudiez, Leon S (New York: Columbia University Press, 1982).

Perlmutter, Dawn. 'The Sacrificial Aesthetic: Blood Rituals From Art To Murder', in *Anthropoetics* 5/2 (1999–2000): 1–20.

Robbins, Tim, director. *Dead Man Walking* (USA: Gramercy Films, 1995).

Sarig, Roni. Review of *The Boatman's Call*. http://www.amazon.co.uk/Boatmans-Call-Nick-Cave/ Accessed 28 August 2007.

Chapter Ten

'It's a Hungry Home': Post-colonial Displacements, Popular Music and the Sacred

> One's implementation in a landscape, one's attachment to Place, without which the universe would become insignificant and would scarcely exist, is the very splitting of humanity into natives and strangers.[1]

> **Great Southern Land**
> Great Southern Land, Great Southern Land
> you walk alone like a primitive man
> and they make it work with sticks and bones
> see their hungry eyes, it's a hungry home . . . [2]

Metaphors of emptiness, distance and desert proliferate in discourses about colonial and post-colonial Australia. However, alongside this deeply entrenched trope, and seemingly conversely, the nation has been steeped in fantasies of being overrun or invaded, and experiences of desperate migration and refuge-seeking. The discourses that have burgeoned around these two recurring tropes inform opposing but linked narratives in the ongoing national preoccupation with what 'home' might signify. What post-colonial scholar Roland Boer describes as 'The thirst, indeed the rage—for a land, a home, an ethnic unity and national or at least group identity'[3] has driven many to perpetrate atrocities on those excluded from the group. In an essay entitled 'Home is always Elsewhere', Boer examines the ways in which the myths and metaphors of home and its counter-

1. Emmanuel Levinas, *Difficult Freedom: Essays on Judaism*, translated by Seán Hand, *Johns Hopkins Jewish Studies*, edited by Sander, Gilman and Katz, Steven T (Baltimore, MD: Johns Hopkins University Press, 1990), 232.
2. Iva Davies, 'Primitive Man', at <www.icehouse-iva.com>. Accessed 19 June, 2006.
3. Roland Boer, *Last Stop before Antarctica: The Bible and Postcolonialism in Australia* (Sheffield: Sheffield Academic Press, 2001), 91.

point, exodus, have informed so many diverse migratory movements: the Dutch in South Africa as Israelites in the desert; the Puritans of America on the way to God's promised land; liberation theology's use of the Exodus myth; the immigrant waves in Australia. In these versions of the myth, he argues, home and expulsion from home depend on each other. Boer invokes what he calls the demonic aspect of the myth, aligning the oppressive uses of the biblical book of Exodus with 'the severity of monotheism, and its demands for one people, one God, one land'.[4] In this he is in agreement with Emmanuel Levinas who saw the ambivalent nature of 'home' as both necessity, and perpetrator of murderous exclusions. This essay asks the following questions: How can home, so often invoked as sacred, as crucible of meaning and identity, be imagined—let alone lived—in the contemporary diasporic world, and in the context of this doubleness and splitting to which Levinas points? Further, in the light of the splitting, and the ambivalence that congeals around 'home', are there be any sacred understandings still possible in the contemporary manias over home/homeland/nation? What kind of sacredness might this be?

So, what is the genealogy of 'home' in relation to two seemingly contradictory paradigms of the contemporary sacred?: first, the sacred as place, belonging, rootedness, identity, relation to land, kinship; and secondly, the sacred as migrant and peripatetic, as seeking, journeying, homeless, offering glimpses but never attaining. In examining these two paradigms of sacredness, we can see that the first is an object, an entity or phenomenon; the second is adjectival, and adjectival of a process; so in fact we are dealing with two different epistemologies: being and becoming. The essay's argument is that it is crucial, in the context of continued global unrest over nationhood and homeland, and the consequent violent displacements of human communities, to continue seeking ways of negotiating between the apparent contradictions of these two paradigms, exemplified in part by the spirit of Wilfred Owen's 'dulce et decorum est pro patria mori' on the one hand, and that embodied in the Judeo-Christian theology of prophets in the desert, of Jesus as nomadic man-god, unacknowledged prophet in his own country, having 'no place to lay his head'.

The argument of this essay focuses on the myths of home and homelessness that have received currency in Australian popular music about and by indigenous Australians. In Australian rock group *Ice House*'s iconic 1982 anthem, 'Great Southern Land', the poetry of Iva Davies is deeply

4. Boer, *Last Stop*, 93.

ambivalent about the place of indigenous Australians and white settlers in what is figured as a 'faraway' land.

'Great Southern Land'

Standing at the limit of an endless ocean
stranded like a runaway, lost at sea
city on a rainy day down in the harbour
watching as the grey clouds shadow the bay
looking everywhere 'cause I had to find you
this is not the way that I remember it here
anyone will tell you its a prisoner island
hidden in the summer for a million years

Great Southern Land, burned you black
so you look into the land and it will tell you a story
story 'bout a journey ended long ago
if you listen to the motion of the wind in the mountains
maybe you can hear them talking like I do
'...they're gonna betray, they're gonna forget you
are you gonna let them take you over this way...'
Great Southern Land, Great Southern Land
you walk alone like a primitive man
and they make it work with sticks and bones
see their hungry eyes, it's a hungry home
I hear the sound of the stranger's voices
I see their hungry eyes, their hungry eyes
Great Southern Land, Great Southern Land
they burned you black, black against the ground

Great Southern Land, in the sleeping sun
you walk alone with the ghost of time
they burned you black, black against the ground
and they make it work with rocks and sand
I hear the sound of the strangers' voices
I see their hungry eyes, their hungry eyes
Great Southern Land, Great Southern Land
you walk alone, like a primitive man
you walk alone with the ghost of time
and they burned you black

yeah, they burned you black
Great Southern Land.[5]

In the lines describing the first white inhabitants, convicts 'standing at the limit of an endless ocean', 'standing' is half-rhymed with 'stranded', in a land where memory is ripped or leached from you. It is a 'prisoner island' where you're 'betrayed and forgotten'. If you listen to this land, the song tells us, its message is at the very least ambivalent: like the strangers who watch you with hungry eyes, you too will become primitive, blackened, devoured by the ghost of time. And the story the land will tell you is that a journey—the archetypal journey of migration and settlement—'ended long ago', presumably a reference to the ancient occupation of the land by indigenous Australians. 'Great Southern Land', written at the beginning of an important decade in Indigenous and non-Indigenous relations, and the politics of land rights, has been considered a pro-Aboriginal song, appearing on play lists repetitively right to the present. However, its ambivalence towards the land and its inhabitants, and its blurring of indigenous and non-indigenous positions, are worth probing.

With its contemporary hymn—or anthem-like rhythm, its chanted chorus, and indigenous background music/sound, it has the movement and the speaking perspective of a walking nomad, but not an indigenous nomad. The speaker of the song's narrative is a white intruder almost overwhelmed in an alien place. However, the unnamed strangers who watch you from the land are described as being able to 'make it work' with sticks and bones, with rocks and sand. The lyrics express ambivalence towards this place, or towards being in this place as an intruder, and the song does not resolve in any simple way. This is because the music beckons, celebrates, declares and repeats the reality of this huge, strange, mythic place: 'Great Southern Land'. When the song appeared in 1982, a torrid decade of political unrest in Australia, culminating in the 1988 Australian Bicentenary celebrations—or mourning—was just beginning. In the song, written and performed by a white band, perspectives of indigenous and non-indigenous are arguably highly ambiguous. The narrator is not indigenous, but 'like a primitive man', an outsider viewing as other those who 'make it work . . . see their hungry eyes, it's a hungry home'.

In the same year, the Australian musician Shane Howard and his less commercial, though hugely popular band, Goanna, recorded the song

5. Icehouse, 'Great Southern Land', *Primitive Man*, (Australia: Regular, 1982), ©2006 at <www.icehouse-iva.com>. Accessed 19 June 2006.

'Solid Rock', an up-tempo, driving rock song with a deeply serious theme. Lyrically a much more overtly political song, 'Solid Rock' registers the ravages of colonialism:

'Solid Rock'

Out here nothin' changes, not in a hurry anyway
You feel the endlessness with the comin' of the light o' day
We're talkin' about a chosen place
You wouldn't sell it in a marketplace, well
Well just a minute now

Standing on solid rock
Standing on sacred ground
Living o-on borrowed soil
And the winds of change are blowin' down the line
Right down the line
Round about the dawn o' time, When dreamin' all began
A crowd o' people came
Well they were looking for their promised land
Were running from the heart of darkness
Searching for the heart o' light
Well it was their paradise

But they were standin' on - solid rock
Standing o-on sacred grou-ound
Living o-on borrowed soil
And the winds of change were blowing cold that night . . . Oh

They were standin' on the shore one day, Saw the white sails in the sun
Wasn't long before they felt the sting, white man, white law, white gun
Don't tell me that it's justified, 'cause somewhere, someone lied
Yeah well someone lied, someone lied, genocide
Well someone lied, oh, ahh
And now you're standing on—solid rock
Standing o-on a sacred grou-ound
Living o-on borrowed soil
And the winds of change are blowin' down the li-ine

Solid rock, Standing on sacred ground
Living o-on borrowed soil

> And the winds of change are blowing down the line
> Solid rock, Standing o-on sacred grou-ound
> Living o-on borrowed ti-i-i-ime
> And the winds of change are blowing down the line
> Oh-oh-oh no, NO-O[6]

Against this theme of uprooting and desecration, the song utopically posits a place of authenticity, a land where nothing changes; it is an endless, chosen place, not able to be sold in the marketplace, a promised land, a heart of light, their paradise, solid rock, sacred ground. While at the level of the lyrics and the narrative the song goes on to undermine the solidity of all these claims of unchanging promise, as the reality of change, cultural commodification and invasion are narrated, it is at the level of the music that the joy of being in place, standing on solid rock, is celebrated and reiterated. But again the fact that this was a white band narrating indigenous locatedness arguably sets up some ambivalence. By the end of 1982 'Solid Rock' was number one on Australian popular music charts and the album *Spirit of Place* had sold 300,000 copies (a large number for the Australian population of eighteen million). 'Solid Rock's' non-Indigenous author and singer described in these words the song's reception when the band went on tour:

> Every town we played, they'd be a group of aboriginal people who would actually come to check out these white fellows, what do those white fellows know about cultures or aboriginality? But we learned very fast, and we learned every night. It meant sitting up till 2, 3 in the morning, talking to groups of aboriginal people in every town we went into. And we were hearing firsthand the stories of how they grew up, the life they had to lead. The oppression and the racism that they lived with every day. And every night when you're hearing direct stories from aboriginal people, once you know, you then can't un-know.[7]

In his 1998 essay 'Geographies of the Sacred and Post-colonial Literatures', in the volume of post-colonial essays entitled *Spirit of Place: Source of the Sacred*, Canadian Jamie Scott writes from a non-indigenous awareness of 'the precariousness of our own sacred contexts, the historical accident of

6. Goanna, 'Solid Rock', *Spirit of Place* (Australia/New Zealand: Wea International), ©1982 Shane Howard.
7. Goanna. 'Solid Rock'.

our own sacred locations . . . in a heightened awareness of the relativity of all locatedness, human or divine'.[8] It is a sense of the sacred, he writes, that honours 'critical practices of dislodgement, without which . . . narratives become fortified places, abiding cities'.[9] This 'relativity of all locatedness' applies most obviously to the second of the descriptions of contemporary sacredness outlined above: the sacred as migrant and peripatetic, as seeking, journeying, homeless, offering glimpses but never attaining.

The argument of this present essay is that sacredness—experienced emotionally, politically, psychologically, spiritually, morally, physically—so often operates in Australia, and in many white settler, colonised countries, with a sharp and simultaneous double sense of home and homelessness; of the importance of acknowledging 'the relativity of all locatedness', even when, or perhaps especially when, we claim to be most at home. Of course the relative weight and the nature of such split experiences of 'home' falls differently for indigenous and non-indigenous in these colonial contexts. For example, in the music, almost against the lyrics, of 'Great Southern Land', and in the rhythmic drive of 'Solid Rock', the dialectic between these two paradigms can be seen at work: desire for home and a sense of the impossibility of home, as mutually implicated ideas; and relatedly, home as built by inclusion, while also necessitating exclusion, to remember Levinas. Is this oscillation between home and homelessness—experienced differently by colonisers and colonised—able to be seen as dialectical, or are we dealing here simply with contradictory and necessarily antagonistic motions? Can the human desire for home, belonging, land, place—so powerfully voiced by Indigenous and diasporic peoples, and differently by colonisers—hold at its heart, in reasoned, social human practices, its opposite, a significant acknowledgement of homelessness, rootlessness, journeying, and the exclusions, expulsions, barriers caused by defending home? What can this dialectical epistemology of home promise to achieve? And what distinctions need to be maintained in regard to colonisers and colonised when thinking about this doubleness?

Homelessness at the heart of 'home' is the central idea of rock band Midnight Oil's famous anthem, 'Beds are Burning', from the 1986 album *Diesel and Dust*. The song was performed most famously at the 2000 Olympics closing ceremony. Midnight Oil's iconic front man, Peter Garrett—tall and shaven-headed, his trademark gangly figure taken over in his contorted, gyrating dance style—is now the Federal Labour for the

8. Scott, 'Geographies of the Sacred', 70.
9. Scott, 'Geographies of the Sacred', 61.

environment. The 2000 Olympics performance of 'Beds are Burning', the group dressed in track suits with 'Sorry' scrawled across various parts of their bodies, was beamed around the world. The song's lyrics were known, mantra-style, by many of the crowd, who sang and danced throughout the performance:

'Beds are Burning'

Out where the river broke
The bloodwood and the desert oak
Holden wrecks and boiling diesels
Steam in forty five degrees

The time has come
To say fair's fair
To pay the rent
To pay our share
The time has come
A fact's a fact
It belongs to them
Let's give it back

How can we dance when our earth is turning
How do we sleep while our beds are burning
How can we dance when our earth is turning
How do we sleep while our beds are burning

The time has come to say fair's fair
to pay the rent, now to pay our share

Four wheels scare the cockatoos
From Kintore East to Yuendemu
The western desert lives and breathes
In forty five degrees

The time has come
To say fair's fair
To pay the rent
To pay our share
The time has come
A fact's a fact
It belongs to them
Let's give it back

How can we dance when our earth is turning
How do we sleep while our beds are burning
How can we dance when our earth is turning
How do we sleep while our beds are burning[10]

The lyrics work powerfully, with their simple, idealistic logic: it is theirs, give it back. The music and lyrics are anthemic, repeated, and call out to the crowd to join in. Behind this emotionally simple logic, and the repeated rhetorical questions—How can we . . . how do we—stands the utterly complicated historical and legal conundrum of land rights in Australia, and thc already grievous loss of languages and traditional forms of life. The powerful central image of burning beds is compounded by the poem's depiction of Australia as unhomely for all but the indigenous inhanbitants, a land of wild heat, floods, wrecked and derelict vehicles. In other words, a land impenetrable—or almost—to modernity. But it is also a home to those who belong, who have adapted: 'The western desert lives and breathes/In forty five degrees.'

The Western Desert, encompassing the Gibson and Great Sandy deserts, is still the traditional country of groups of Pintupi, Warlpiri and Martu Aboriginals. Pushed out of their traditional forms of living in the 1960s by the Menzies government's assimilationist policies, these groups have since been 'settled' in mixed Aboriginal communities such as Papunya, Hermannsburg and Haasts Bluff in The Northern Territory, between the 1960s and the 1980s. The Western Desert, or Papunya Tula Art movement, now internationally famous for the so-called 'dot paintings', originated in this country 240 kilometres west of Alice Springs. The 2002 Philip Noyce film *Rabbit Proof Fence*, based on the novel/memoir *Molly's Daughter* by Doris Pilkington Garimara, is also set through this country. Most white settler Australians have not visited these parts of Australia, but communities such as Kintore East and Yuendemu have a mythic resonance for many. Four-wheel drive vehicles obviously also penetrate out there.

In June 2004, left-wing, radical political commentator Margot Kingston wrote a typically larrikin and subversive article entitled 'Howard's Memory of burning beds' for the *Sydney Morning Herald*, recalling the Oils' Olympic event. With no love lost between herself and the Australian Prime Minister John Howard, and with no pretence of journalistic objectivity, Kingston quotes web diarist Mark Hayes:

10. Midnight Oil, 'Beds are Burning', *Diesel and Dust* (Australia: Sony Music, 1986). ©1986 Midnight Oil Music and Sony Music Australia.

> Remember back in August 2000, when the Olympics were on after hundreds of thousands of Australians showed their support for Aboriginal Reconciliation though the famous bridge walks and seas of hands? The Prime Minister had, and has, refused to apologise and say 'Sorry' to the Aboriginal people.
>
> At the closing ceremony of the Games— that huge stadium party and concert broadcast live around the world to an audience of over one billion people—Midnight Oil, dressed in black track suits with the word 'Sorry' stencilled on them, ripped into 'Beds are Burning' before an ecstatic crowd.
>
> Yothu Yindi followed up with 'Treaty'.
>
> The crowd at Olympic Stadium went berserk in screaming support, knowing exactly what was being done to shame the Government over Reconciliation. Sitting in the audience with nowhere to run or hide, and no 'I am advised' to scuttle behind, Prime Minister Howard had no choice but to squirm and receive the huge, public, 'F . . . You' delivered loudly, proudly, and strongly by the Oils and Yothu Yindi.
>
> He never forgets any slight delivered upon him, and exacts revenge whenever and wherever possible. This was a massive public rebuke at his meanness. And he won't ever forget it.[11]

That's why his favourite Oils song is 'Beds are Burning', and he won't sleep while his bed is burning for revenge against Labor for publicly embracing Peter Garrett, who delivered that most public of attacks on John Howard at what should have been one of his triumphant moments.

This indeed was an odd moment in Australian Indigenous/White Settler relations. The Prime Minister, not known for his popular culture involvement, responded to the leading question 'What is your favourite Midnight Oil song' in the context of the Olympics, causing much ironic amusement. The very idea of white Australia being in debt to its Aboriginal inhabitants, or of rental due, is anathema to most conservative Australians, and certainly to the present Federal government.

Another Midnight Oil song, 'Maralinga', written by Garrett and Oil's guitarist Jim Monginie, appears on the 1982 album *10, 9, 8, 7, 6, 5, 4, 3, 2, 1.* It is a spoken song, in the voice of an Aboriginal person witnessing the horrors of British nuclear testing at Maralinga, on the Nullabor Plain of Western Australia. Much has been written about the tests, and

11. Margot Kingston, 'Howard's Memory of burning beds', in *Sydney Morning Herald online,* Accessed 14 June 2004. *http://www.smh.com.au/articles/2004/06/14/1087065071551.html*

their ongoing legacy, conducted in 1956 (Operation Buffalo) and 1957 (Operation Antler), on land which was considered sacred to the Pitjantjatjara and Yankunytjatjara peoples. The opening lines of the song come from a displaced voice remembering home: 'I come from a land of wide open spaces/Where the world turns around us and we just follow suit.' The transformation of a whole way of life is sudden and apocalyptic:

> In the wind
> The ashes fly
> The poison crown
> The charcoal ground
>
> And if you can't see the smile in me, that's where I wanna be . . .
> There's only God
>
> There's only Christ
> Think I'll lie down for just a while . . .[12]

The land turns from an environment lived in for centuries, to 'charcoal ground'. The reference to 'The poison crown' of course invokes the newly acquired 'Crown Land', and British power; as do the references to God and Christ, as the new British overlords. Again, home is made horrifically unhomely, in the name of gods and powers unheard of by those who were dispossessed:

> And the grass became granite
> And the sky a black sheet
> Our bed was a graveyard
> We couldn't feel our blistered feet . . .[13]

But what is most uncanny and moving about the lyrics of 'Maralinga' is that the speaker, who watches the awful sublimity of the nuclear tests, and their effects on the land, wants to be there, in country:

> All around
> An eerie sound
> Their dreams a cloud
> Their world in shrouds

---

12. Midnight Oil, 'Maralinga', *10, 9, 8, 7, 6, 5, 4, 3, 2, 1* (Australia: Sony Music, 1982), ©1982 Midnight Oil Music and Sony Music Australia.
13. Midnight Oil, 'Maralinga'.

In the wind
The ashes fly
Not much time
But time to try
And if you can't see the smile in me, that's cos I wanna be
I want to be here at the end. I have to be here at the end.[14]

The mesmeric phantasm of nuclear explosion—'Their dreams a cloud/ Their world in shrouds/in the wind'—draws the speaker into the apocalypse, to be there even 'at the end'. The sorrow of the speaker is caused because this is a traditional custodian of place speaking. He marks the awful transformation, unable to smile. The awful gap between European dreams of land use for modern, experimental purposes, and the urgent, need of the custodian to be once again in country opens up at this point. He will, if ever he makes it back, be in country at the same time as that country has been transformed into utter unhomeliness.

For indigenous Australians, homelessness—loss of languages, loss of traditional country, loss of memory and community—has been thrust upon them, and continues to be so. The dialectic between home and homelessness, voiced in the lyrics of 'Maralinga', has its own trajectory for Indigenous Australians, emerging out of deeply traditional relationship to the land, to ancestors, and to dreamings. But this dialectic is different for White Australians. In 2007, the long hard processes of coming to understand homelessness as something which they have perpetrated—upon the land and upon its first inhabitants—are now reaching maturity. Since the June 3, 1992 Mabo High Court decision for the Meriam People, and the first white settler awakenings to the nonsense that was the doctrine of terra nullius, multiple land claims have been proceeding, with varying results, across the country. However, life expectancy, infant mortality, education levels, incarceration and suicide rates are still much worse than for white Australians, and the health conditions and employment prospects of many Indigenous individuals and communities are still at disgraceful, internationally queried levels of poverty.

So, what is the particular dynamic that needs to be acknowledged and worked through for white Australians, now? Is it possible for white Australia, looking into the distorted mirror of Australia's history, to see both the ongoing Aboriginal dispossession and to see its own face reflected, but differently, transformatively? The argument of this essay is that to do

14. Midnight Oil, 'Maralinga'.

so, and to continue the processes of renewal and justice, it is necessary for non-Indigenous Australians to learn to think and practice 'home' and 'dislodgement' together. The songs of the early 1980s were already alive to such a need. Such a double understanding acknowledged at a national level would be truly post-colonial.

A richly poetic exemplar of such thinking can be found, as early as 1966, in the poetry of post-colonial poet Judith Wright. Her poem, 'A Document', is the work of a privileged daughter of pastoral landowners who had settled in the fertile New England area of New South Wales. Wright, whose life's work across the 1950s to the 1980s would lead her to personally devastating realisations about her own role in the dispossession of Indigenous Australia, wrote 'A Document', a paean of love to the country she knew and had grown up in. But it is a poem that also represents the dawning awareness that home must, from that time on, always carry the double freight of love and displacement:

'A Document'

'Sign there.' I signed, but still uneasily.
I sold the coachwood forest in my name.
Both had been given me; but all the same
remember that I signed uneasily.

Ceratopetalum, Scented Satinwood:
a tree attaining seventy feet in height.
Those pale-red calyces like sunset light
burned in my mind. a flesh-pink pliant wood

used in coachbuilding. Difficult of access
(those slopes were steep). But it was World War Two.
Their wood went into bomber-planes. They grew
hundreds of years to meet those hurried axes.

Under our socio-legal dispensation
both name and woodland had been given me.
I was much younger then than any tree
matured for timber. But to help the nation

I signed the document. The stand was pure
(eight hundred trees perhaps). Uneasily

> (the bark smells sweetly when you wound the tree)
> I set upon this land my signature.[15]

Here we are given the intimate details of the land, and the speaker's love of it: the coachwood forest, '*Ceratopetalum,* Scented Satinwood', 'they grew/ hundreds of years', 'the stand was pure', 'the bark smells sweetly when you wound the tree'.[16] Latin abuts with sensuous new-world knowledge and descriptors, as a retrospective but active, poetic meaning-making takes place. Home is both the loved intimacy of forests and childhood memories, and it is the place given her 'Under our socio-legal dispensation'; it is part of the nation.

Some readers might identify guilt and regret here, in the realization of what was done, but the poem encompasses something much more dynamic than mere guilt. There is self-forgiveness—'I signed uneasily', 'I was much younger'—together with a broader social understanding of profound injustice and destruction, performed under the authority of the conquerors: 'I set upon this land my signature'. The uneasy conjoining of deeply private guilt and sorrow, together with public responsibility, has the effect of a shock. Ownership and rights are placed beside a wounding loss, as the pure stand of eight hundred trees turns into bomber planes for the war, for the nation. The personal and the individual are registered as having public, national import; and the manacles of history are seen to tie down even the person of good will.

However, what opens the poem up to moving beyond the merely personal and nostalgic thoughts of a white settler Australian, is the forthright and passionate disposition towards justice being registered by the individual voice. Wright traces her own love of land, but also the need to re-read and re-understand such love, in the light of present realities. It is a moment, this poem, which births an awareness of what British theologian Rowan Williams describes as time and understanding belonging together, and of the power of language to constantly remake. Williams, in the course of an essay on language and sacred belief from the volume *Shadow of Spirit: Postmodernism and Religion* writes:

> What is thinkable is so precisely because thinking is not content with the abstraction of mutual exclusivities, but struggles to con-

15. Judith Wright, 'A Document', in *Collected Poems 1942–1970* (Sydney: Angus & Robertson, 1971), 244.
16. Wright, 'A Document', 244.

> ceive a structured wholeness nuanced enough to contain what appeared to be contradictories. Once again: time and understanding belong together; language constantly remakes itself in the fact of what is not yet understood, criticizes itself unceasingly . . . we can indeed abstract to the trace of a perpetual shadow . . . but this shadow *can only 'appear'* in the historical process of making (communicable, communal) sense, in the 'following' of discourse.[17]

Williams is here speaking into the dialectic of being and becoming in an original way. While his desire for 'wholeness nuanced enough to contain what appeared to be contradictories' might be dismissed by some as naively utopian, his theorised and pragmatic understanding of the operations of language is gripping and persuasive: language as always capable of both abstraction and communicability, of approaching the mysterious, the 'not yet understood', the place of the shadow; but it also carries a desire to make the future, to communicate, to commune. Williams sees language as richly philosophical in its impossible reaching out towards something contradictory and beyond reach; but also as the humble tool of particular times and understandings, particular communities and places when moments of reconciliation, healing, home might be urgently needed and achievable. What can Williams' delineation of this dual capacity and practice of language do to assist thought and practice of 'home' in Australia?

Like Williams, Australian critic Jennifer Rutherford is interested in intervening in monolithic understandings of home and nation, but she approaches these questions in different ways. Instead of focussing on the possibilities of language, she seeks to disrupt unified mythologies that paper thinly over deeper, psychic struggles for home. In her cultural and literary analysis of Australia, *The Gauche Intrude*, she focuses on 'the way that fantasies of the good provide a camouflage for aggression at both a national and local level: an aggression directed both to an external and an internal Other'.[18] For Rutherford, following novelist Patrick White's infamous 1950s description of Australia as 'the Great Australian Emptiness', she argues that the good, homey, egalitarian nation of Australia needs to recognise the spiritual dimension of its emptiness, an emptiness which is

17. RowanWilliams, 'Hegel and the Gods of Postmodernity', in *Shadow of Spirit: Postmodernism and Religion*, edited by Philipa Berry, and Andrew Wernick (London and New York: Routledge, 1992), 76.
18. Jennifer Rutherford, *The Gauche Intruder: Freud, Lacan and the White Australian Fantasy* (Melbourne: Melbourne University Press, 2000), 10.

> . . . an aggression towards the Other that has been endemic in white Australian history; the fantasy of the good neighbour and the good nation that has sustained this aggression; and a certain experience of emptiness, of a symbolic fragility or inequality to the task of representing this nothingness, that fantasy has never been able to occlude.[19]

This is written by Rutherford well before the Tampa 'incident', when a boat carrying refugees ('illegal immigrants', 'queue jumpers') was intercepted off the coast of Western Australia; and it is written well before official responses to the death of all 353 refugees on another boat, the SIEV X, close to Australian shores. *The Gauche Intruder* is alive to the power of national myths, and of the rhetorical and political mechanisms actively constructing such myths. Rutherford places in linguistic, literary and psychoanalytic terms what happens when we buy our own rhetoric, when home becomes the monolithic, protected, expulsive refusal of others, even as it dresses itself up in the very terms of protection of the nation, home, kith and kin; in other words, when home is mandated as this 'splitting of humanity into natives and strangers',[20] rather than the double, dialectic sense, for post-colonial citizens, of homelessness within all understandings of home.

In this context, the lyrics of the fifth and final song addressed in this essay, 'Treaty', from the 1991 album *Tribal Voice* by Aboriginal (Yolnu) Band Yothu Yindi are significant. 'Yothu Yindi' means in Gumatj, the Yolnu tribal language, 'child and mother'. The song's lyrics can be read as a particular instance of thinking home and displacement dialectically, first painfully and realistically for Indigenous Australians, but also in calling white Australia to respond. 'Treaty' is politically, emotionally, musically and poetically alive to love of home, and the fact that the dream of home will continually be erased. The song is utopian in the richest understanding of that word, dealing with a full and powerful sense of the particularity of place—'country' that has been lived in for 40,000 years. Yet the song also comprehends the deeply precarious, unabiding nature of home, and the fact that no-one—Indigenous and non-indigenous alike—*owns* the land. The song declares that 'words are easy, words are cheap', but it also simultaneously *uses* words—English and Gumatj—and music, to dream

19. Jennifer Rutherford, *The Gauche Intruder*, 12.
20. Levinas, *Difficult Freedom*, 232.

up home and its loss. The very necessity for a treaty points to this double understanding of home and its precariousness:

'Treaty'

Well I heard it on the radio
And I saw it on the television
Back in 1988
All those talking politicians
Words are easy, words are cheap
Much cheaper than our priceless land
But promises can disappear
Just like writing in the sand

Treaty Yeh Treaty Now
Treaty Yeh Treaty Now
Nhima Djatpangarri nhima walangwalang–
Nhe Djatpayatpa nhima gaya nhe-
Matjini . . . Yakarray—nhe Djat'pa nhe walang—Gumurrtijararrk
Gutjuk–

This land was never given up
This land was never bought and sold
The planting of the Union Jack
Never changed our law at all

Now two rivers run their course
Separated for so long
I'm dreaming of a brighter day
When the waters will be one

Treaty Yeh Treaty Now Treaty Yeh Treaty Now
Treaty Yeh Treaty Now Treaty Yeh Treaty Now
Nhima djatpa nhe walang
gumurrtjararrk yawirriny Nhe gaya nhe matjini
Gaya nhe matjini Gaya gaya nhe gaya nhe
Matjini walangwalang Nhema djatpa nhe walang—Nhe gumurrt-
jarrk nhe ya-

Promises—Disappear—Priceless land—Destiny–
Well I heard it on the Radio - And I saw it on the Television
But promises can be broken
Just like writing in the sand

Treaty Yeh
Treaty Now . . .[21]

At the literal level this can be seen as a hardnosed, political cry—we know you colonisers lie, so give us a treaty. The song jams utopian, emotional 'truth' up against political pragmatism: 'This land was never given up/ This land was never bought and sold/ The planting of the Union Jack / Never changed our law at all', and is thus, in its self-conscious fictionalising, both a poignant overreaching, and an exhilarating challenge to make such claims true. There is a double understanding of language here: an acknowledgment that history is written in language, and language can have at its heart an emptiness and duplicity. But there is also the grasping of a more processual, local, temporary and communicable use of language, analogous to Jamie Scott and Rowan Williams' understandings of the sacred, a figuring of home and dislodgement in continual, dialectical, questioning negotiation with each other.

This essay has argued that it is in particular contexts, and ceaselessly, dialectically, with a double awareness of homelessness within home, that post-colonial Australian understandings of home need to be forged. The cry for a treaty can be read as pragmatic, coming from a merely political understanding of the need for legal certitude, but that is not the overwhelming effect of this song by Yothu Yindi. From somewhere at the heart of its mix of indigenous and white musical technologies, its use of Gumatj and English, it oscillation between fragile utopian desire and a hardnosed call for legal structures, a sacred impulse has been felt and shared by many who hear the song (all Australians, arguably). The song embodies an impulse, a pulse, finding ways to express deep desire for home, as well as a transforming realisation that such desires need to acknowledge—vulnerably, hauntedly, dialectically—the 'relativity of all locatedness'.

Do such claims to relativity finally neutralise any political, practical claims to home and country by indigenous and post-colonial in Australia; or worse, do they belong to a stagnant, nostalgic insistence on return to an unattainable past? On the contrary, this essay has been arguing that it is Indigenous Australians, and those artists and audiences who respond to them, who are most acutely aware of this claim to home which persists amongst all the different kinds of homelessness in post-colonial Australia. Across a multitude of pragmatic and metaphoric levels, for colonised

21. Yothu Yindi, 'Treaty', *Tribal Voice* (Australia: Mushroom, 1991), ©1991 Mushroom and Yothu Yindi.

and colonisers, holding together the human need for home with an understanding of the constant reality of human dislocatedness is a riven, necessary and unending process. Openness to such processes for making 'home' is urgently needed in the political languages of negotiation, in poetic and musical expressions, and in personal and public discourses of home in Australia. Such openness can be described as a sacred quality, in an understanding of the contemporary post-colonial sacred as migrant and peripatetic, a continuing journey in search of home.

Works Cited

Boer, Roland. *Last Stop before Antarctica: The Bible and Postcolonialism in Australia* (Sheffield: Sheffield Academic Press, 2001).

The Age, 4 December 2002, (http://www.theage.com.au/articles/2002/).

Goanna. 'Solid Rock' (song), *Spirit of Place*, Australia/New Zealand: *Wea International*. Copyright © 1982 Shane Howard.

---- *The Music of Goanna* website: http://members.aol.com/boardwalk7/goanna.

Grabosky, PN. (1985) 'A toxic legacy : British nuclear weapons testing in Australia', in *Wayward governance: Illegality and its Control in the Public Sphere* (Canberra: Australian Institute of Criminology, 1985), 235–253.

Icehouse 'Great Southern Land' (song), *Primitive Man*, 1982. Australia: Regular. ©2006 www.icehouse-iva.com.

Kingston, Margot, 'Howard's Memory of burning beds', in *Sydney Morning Herald* online, Accessed 14 June 2004.
http://www.smh.com.au/articles/2004/06/14/1087065071551.html

Levinas, Emmanuel. *Difficult Freedom: Essays on Judaism,* translated Hand, Sean. *Johns Hopkins Jewish Studies,* edited by Gilman, Sander and Katz, Steven T (Baltimore, MD: Johns Hopkins University Press, 1990).

Midnight Oil. 'Beds are Burning' (song), *Diesel and Dust*, Copyright © 1986 Midnight Oil Music Copyright © Sony Music Australia.

----'Maralinga' (song) 1982, *10, 9, 8, 7, 6, 5, 4, 3, 2, 1*, Copyright © 1982 Midnight Oil Music Copyright © Sony Music Australia.

Rutherford, Jennifer. *The Gauche Intruder: Freud, Lacan and the White Australian Fantasy* (Melbourne: Melbourne University Press, 2000).

Scott, Jamie S. 'Geographies of the Sacred and Post-colonial Literatures', edited by Griffith, Michael and Tulip, James. *Spirit of Place: Source of the Sacred* (Sydney: Berget, 1998), 50–74.

Williams, Rowan. 'Hegel and_the Gods of_Postmodernity', *Shadow of Spirit: Postmodernism and Religion*, edited by Berry, Philippa and Wernick, Andrew (London and New York: Routledge, 1992), 72–80.

Wright, Judith. 'A Document', *Collected Poems 1942–1970* (Sydney: Angus & Robertson, 1971), 244.

Yothu Yindi. 'Treaty' (song), 1991 *Tribal Voice*, Australia: Mushroom © Yothu Yindi.

Chapter Eleven

Sacred Violence in the Chamberlain Case

The scapegoat

In the early 1980s many Australians demanded their say about 'Lindy Chamberlain'. On radio, in letters to the media, over coffee and on television, we exposed our wisdoms about mothering, matricide, inappropriate family holiday destinations, religious sects, the dressing of children in black, the desert, the law, and the requirements of justice. Australians—not for the first time—eagerly devoured tales of uncanny happenings in the desert. In the heart of the county, at Ayers Rock as it was still called, a sacrifice of some kind had occurred. 'Why would you take a child out there?' 'As if a dingo could do that!'

At the centre of the maelstrom was the small, determined figure of a woman. The factors which singled out Lindy Chamberlain from the very beginning were her gender and her religion. Her gender, or the way she was perceived to perform it, was seen increasingly as truculent, not sufficiently grief-stricken, not meek or repentant in the face of growing media and legal accusations against her. Further, the Chamberlains' membership of what mainstream Australia saw as a 'strange', imported religious group, The Seventh Day Adventists, soon became a source of intrigue and some derision to the general public. Not seen as a cult, quite, this barely understood American religious group and the Chamberlains' membership of it was deemed different and suspicious.

Within this context of increasingly flamboyant media constructions—a gothic, violent outback setting that even today lives within myths of frontier lawlessness, paganism, and racial atrocities—the figure of Lindy Chamberlain rose up as scapegoat. Woman as good or evil Mother, as strong or hardened, as one of 'us' or a stranger in our midst—no image of Lindy Chamberlain was produced which could not be twisted into the shape of its opposite. In the gathering clouds of 'hearsay' and 'judgment',

Australian society was, perhaps half-knowingly, enacting a sacred and ancient ritual, offering up one for the whole.

In 2004, Di Drew, director of the two-part miniseries *Through My Eyes*, based on the Chamberlain case, reported that when she spoke about Lindy Chamberlain to groups of friends, or to the extras on set, asking whether they thought Lindy (as many called her) guilty or innocent, '. . . the response was usually the same: the group divides 65/35 per cent, with the majority verdict being guilty'. For Drew this was amazing, and she reflects on the ways in which myth accrues around history and everyday normality: 'It was all about that landscape and that place. It was about spirituality and it's been about religion, and a baby's name, and behaviour that's not typical.'[1]

However, for John Bryson, author of the book-length study *Evil Angels*, also later made into a film, such behaviours were not *atypical*; nor were the many so-called scientific biases and mistakes made across the years since that night, 17 August 1980. They are for him the product of culture. In a sharply positioned piece in the *Sydney Morning Herald* in 1995, after the belated inquest into the whereabouts of the body of Azaria Chamberlain, Bryson wrote:

> Once the laboratory mistakes are all swept away, the witnesses left standing have human faces . . . this third finding is a product of its culture, as are judgments of any kind. In that culture, we watch a fascinating mechanism at work: it's something like an inability to retrace one's steps, whatever the cost, or however wrong the path was.[2]

This essay explores the nature of this 'fascinating mechanism', asking how culturally typical was the behaviour of those intimately involved in the Chamberlain case, and of those more far-flung but still somehow drawn into the drama. The case reminds us of the potency of myth, and of ritual, the uses to which they are put in supposedly secular, political contexts. Myths—and stereotypes—about women in many cultures—damned whores and god's police, Mary the mother of God and Mary Magdalene, in myth a prostitute; women as dirty, and women as pure, or at least sent to clean. Further, the essay will argue that responses to the Chamberlain

1. Debi Enker, 'Trial by Fury', in *Sydney Morning Herald*, 22/1/2004, *The Guide*, 4.
2. John Bryson, 'The search for a culprit continues' in *Sydney Morning Herald*, 16/12/1995, *News and Features*, 21.

case, and particularly to the figure of Lindy Chamberlain, need to be read within a context of sacredness, ritual and scapegoating, concepts with disturbing connotations for many in the supposedly deeply secular nation of Australia. The Lindy Chamberlain case opens up the intimate link that exists between the sacred and violence—as the world crashes down, woman will descend and sweep up the shards; or, differently, it has all gone wrong, it must be *her* fault. Not only is the Chamberlain case readable within such a context, but much of the import of what happened to this woman and her family *needs* to be examined in relation to the category of the sacred, as a way of thinking further through the often rancorous divide between sacred and secular in Australian culture.

Sacred and profane

While secularity has its own history, and cannot be reduced to 'the profane', it is important firstly to examine the division between the realms of the sacred and the profane which structure early twentieth century anthropological thinking. In Émile Durkheim's *The Elementary Forms of Religious Life,*[3] Rudolf Otto's *The Idea of the Holy*[4] and Mircea Eliade's *The Sacred and the Profane,*[5] the realm of the sacred was articulated as separate from the profane world of everyday, domestic and ordinary existence, though impinging upon it as an archaic force. In Durkheim's work this power was life-giving and necessary to individuals and society, but could also be ambiguous and even dangerous. Otto built on Durkheim's notion of the anti-rational power of the sacred, locating it 'beyond' the profane and employing certain elements of the sublime, including dread and awe in response to the sacred. For Durkheim, the sacred operated in society through the setting aside of specific times, places, actions (rituals of sacrifice and blood-letting, cleansing, purifying, etc) and objects (totems, emblems), which maintained for the clan a separation of sacred and profane.

For Mary Douglas too, writing several decades later, ritual was at the core of understanding the relations between sacred and profane. In Doug-

3. Emile Durkheim, *The Elementary Forms of Religious Life*, translated by Joseph Swain (London: Allen and Unwin, 1963).
4. Rudolf Otto, *The Idea of the Holy: An Inquiry into the Non-rational Factor in the Idea of the Divine and its Relation to the Rational*, translated by John W Harvey (New York: Oxford University Press, 1950).
5. Mircea Eliade, *The Sacred and the Profane: The Nature of Religion*, translated by Willard R Trask (New York: Harcourt Brace Jovanovich, 1957).

las's canonical work *Purity and Danger*,[6] based on her field work in the Belgian Congo (1949–51 and 1953), she is concerned with understanding the rules a culture establishes in order to decide what is clean and what unclean, what is to be considered holy and what untouchable. In relation to the foundations of ongoing Jewish cultural rules regarding what can and cannot be eaten, and what is constituted as clean, Douglas wrote: 'A rule of avoiding anomalous things affirms and strengthens the definitions to which they do not conform.'[7] Douglas' work continued this concern with borders and definitions, asking how and why it is that peoples need to classify, and to ritualise those classifications. Developing her understandings of taboos and cleanliness in overtly religious societies, she extended these cultures' need for classification and ritual, applying her findings to all societies, writing:

> As a social animal, man is a ritual animal. If ritual is suppressed in one form, it crops up in others, more strongly the more intense the social interaction . . . Social rituals create a reality which would be nothing without them. It is not too much to say that ritual is more to society than words are to thought.[8]

Hence, Douglas's work elaborated upon the sacred aspects of ritual, taboo, anomaly, and conformity to the group, across both religious and so-called secular societies, understanding that cultures need to establish what is acceptable and necessary for order, as against what must be eradicated as anomalous. Ritual, and the raw, instinctual nature of the processes which impel such rituals of recrimination and bloodletting, were certainly evident in the Chamberlain case.

Like Douglas, philosopher René Girard has been influential in questioning this earlier dichotomy of sacred and profane. His seminal texts *Violence and the Sacred* and *The Scapegoat* contribute in specific ways to understanding the Chamberlain case. What are most pertinent are Girard's insights into the relationships between *sacredness, violence* and *sacrifice*, read, with Douglas, as pertaining not just to other, past or so-called primitive societies, but in the urban, western cultures of today.

For Girard, social violence must be understood as a central, sacred and structuring element of social life. Girard argues:

---

6. Mary Douglas, *Purity and Danger* (New York: Routledge, 2002).
7. Douglas, *Purity and Danger*, 41.
8. Douglas, *Purity and Danger*, 63.

> . . . the operations of violence and the sacred are ultimately the same process. Although ethnologists are generally disposed to acknowledge that violence exists at the heart of the sacred, they also hasten to add that the sacred includes another, more important and directly contradictory element . . . it involves order as well as disorder, peace as well as war, creation as well as destruction . . . the theory of generative violence permits us to define the sacred in simple, concrete terms . . . Nonviolence appears as the gratuitous gift of violence . . . men are only capable of reconciling their differences at the expense of a third party . . . the surrogate victim.[9]

In conjoining the violent and sacred practices of many cultures through history, Girard also (controversially) introduces the pan-historical role of the scapegoat and of communal sacrifice. He asks how communities, when they are undergoing particular forms of violence—whether from nature, or between warring groups, or because of an individual's actions—found stability and equilibrium again. Girard describes what he calls 'generative unanimity', understood as 'a process for changing bad violence into stability and fecundity . . . in the attenuated form of ritual sacrifice'.[10] It is in this reading of the workings of the sacred that the role of a surrogate victim arises.

Of course Girard's interpretive agendas need to be acknowledged from the outset. He makes his claims regarding the role of the scapegoat and of ritual within a larger—and in many aspects quite radical—Christian context which acknowledges the centrality of Christ who ' . . . offered us a new historical possibility for breaking the underlying structure of violence'.[11] As his critics have argued, it is sometimes unclear whether Girard's claims are really historical and scientific, and how much they are metaphorical or psychological. As one critic of Girard's *Things Hidden since the Foundation of the World* (1987) writes:

> . . . when he seeks to ground his psychological insights within a literal historical framework, he becomes insensitive to the complexities of the religious symbolization process. By insisting that there literally must be a 'founding murder' as origin of sacrificial

9. René Girard, *Violence and the Sacred* (London and New York: Continuum, 2005), 273.
10. Girard, *Violence and the Sacred*, 280–81.
11. Thomas V Peterson, '*Things Hidden Since the Foundation of the World* by René Girard', in *Journal of the American Academy of Religion*, 57/3 (1989): 642.

ritual, he artificially separates human symbolizing from historical phenomena.[12]

Ordinary Australia

My argument rests strongly on the psychological and metaphoric resonances of Girard's ideas. It is irrefutable that such processes of scapegoating, with all their tragic dimensions, were set in train around the Chamberlain case. The complicating factor—of bad violence turned into stability—described by Girard in positive, Christian terms in regard to a society's need for ritual, can be seen operating, but askew, in this case. Australians—supposedly laconic, secular, not given to the genre of high tragedy, but more usually of comedy or self-parody—found themselves embroiled in a narrative which horrified and fascinated: sacrifice, a child's death, maternal guilt, an ancient desert setting which provoked wild characterizations and judgments. A grand moral and existential battle was initiated juridically and in the media, on the back of an 'ordinary' Australian family.

In the name of justice, Australians from many different places and backgrounds wanted their say, and their say, it seemed, demanded a culprit, legal intervention, a scapegoat, and retribution. It was almost as if it was every Australian's right and duty to have something to say, and this something was usually of a moral, and/or judicial nature. The dingo and black sacrifice jokes came a little later. This phenomenon of nationwide opinionising highlights the core cultural contradiction: in the name of communal justice and stability an avalanche of violent and scapegoating media articles, television programmes, and legal processes were unleashed on the head of a woman. How far can we interpret this avalanche of attention and involvement in the case, from right around the country, as well as internationally, as an enactment of ancient, sacred rituals of scapegoating; as evidence of a deep need to keep the borders of social stability patrolled, the role of the woman and the family in place, the sanctity of motherhood fixed?

Lindy Chamberlain was fixed: as a Seventh Day Adventist, the wife of a preacher, from the highly religious community of Cooranbong, near Avondale, NSW, where there was a Seventh Day Adventist theological college and five Seventh Day Adventist churches, one with over 1000 mem-

12. Peterson, '*Things Hidden*', 642.

bers, in a small area. Not much was known by the broader Australian society about Seventh Day Adventists then, but it was soon broadcast that they were vegetarians, that they did not drink coffee, tea or alcohol, and that they officially adhered to strict laws of justice and personal righteousness. For Adventists, Jesus was believed to have removed himself from earth at his death, and to be doing 'investigative judgment' on all who would make a claim to be admitted to heaven. Americans Ellen G White and her husband James were discussed in public forums as prophets of the Seventh Day Adventist movement: they had lived in Australia, in the Avondale area, and had chosen under God's directions the site of the theological college. Such background 'facts' began to circulate about Lindy Chamberlain and her family's religious history. Secular Australia was in a frenzy.

Within this national frenzy, a litany of strange 'facts' and moral opinions, still able to be recited today by many Australians, began to circulate via the media and from person to person: the child had been named 'Azaria' which meant 'sacrifice in the desert'; Lindy had been known to dress the baby in black, with connotations of Satanism or witchery for some pundits; the deed had been committed in a strange, even haunted place, Ayers Rock (Uluru), where Aborigines were making what to non-indigenous Australians sounded like wild claims about sacred connections to the country, and the Rock. What kind of woman would take her children out to such a place—and such a young child at that? The buzz of suspicion soon grew deafening across the country, and Lindy Chamberlain was transformed, little by little, from suffering mother to perpetrator.

The female monster and her society

In the public embrace of these religious 'facts' and opinions, Chamberlain was transmogrified even further from woman to some other kind of *creature*: doing her nails in court, refusing to cry in public, affectless. The discourses that began to emerge around her raised questions about whether she was a real mother, a real woman, a normal Australian. In this context we must ask again: 'What is a scapegoat?' Girard describes the nature of the ritual victim:

> If the victim is to polarize the aggressive tendencies of the community and effect their transfer to himself (sic), continuity must be maintained. There must be a 'metonymic' relationship between members of the community and ritual victims. There must also be discontinuity. The victim must be neither too familiar to the com-

> munity nor too foreign to it . . . this ambiguity is essential to the cathartic function of the sacrifice.[13]

While critics such as Martha Reineke has criticised Girard for the lack of gender concerns in his universalising and pan-historical anthropology,[14] Girard's analysis of the processes of the sacred and of societal demands for sacrificial victims is still, arguably, enormously helpful and suggestive as we observe the Chamberlain case. Do we, in this case, detect 'a collective transference against a collective victim that can be completely arbitrary and against whom all tensions are projected, the scapegoat'.[15] Some would argue that the legal and communal processes that 'established' Lindy Chamberlain as guilty were not completely arbitrary, yet in hindsight they take on an awful, arbitrary logic: the woman as scapegoat. Julia Kristeva's gendered intervention on the nature of the sacred does move us one step further in thinking about the context of the Chamberlain case:

Could the sacred be, whatever its variants, a two-sided formation? One aspect founded by murder, and the social bond made up of murder's guilt-ridden atonement, with all the projective mechanisms and obsessive rituals that accompany it; and another aspect, like a lining, more secret still and invisible, non-representable, oriented toward those uncertain spaces of unstable identity, toward the fragility—both threatening and fusional—of the archaic dyad, toward the non-separation of subject/object, on which language has no hold but one woven of fright and repulsion?[16]

Kristeva in *Powers of Horror*[17] introduces gender and the archaic dyad—the mother and child—into her discussion of sacredness and scapegoating. She also suggests an even more primal origin to this figure of woman—woman as the one who will always already be *both* source of identity and meaning, *and* of defilement, abjection, loss of stability. Kristeva, drawing on Freudian and Nietszchean notions of archaic violence, here distinguishes between the socio-political realities of violence and its

13. Girard, René. *Violence and the Sacred*, 286.
14. Martha J Reineke, 'The Mother in Mimesis: Kristeva and Girard on Violence and the Sacred', in *Body/Text in Julia Kristeva: Religion, Women, and Psychoanalysis*, edited by David R Crownfield (Albany: State University of New York Press, 1992), 67–85.
15. Girard quoted in Markus Müller, 'Interview with René Girard', in *Anthropoetics* II/1 (June 1996) at <www.anthropoetics.ucla.edu/AP0201/interv.htm>. Accessed April 2005.
16. Julia Kristeva, *In the Beginning Was Love: Psychoanalysis and Faith*, translated by Arthur Goldhammer (New York: Columbia University Press, 1987), 58.
17. Julia Kristeva, *Powers of Horror* (New York: Columbia University Press, 1982).

ritual assuaging, on the one hand, and a more linguistic and psychological understanding of the primal human condition, formed through the dyad of mother and child, and before language, representability, identity. This latter state she describes as causing 'fright and repulsion' in the proper, law-abiding world of discrete representations, of right and wrong, he and she, murderer and innocent. By extension, the scapegoat in Kristeva's frame must be the abject creature par excellence, passing from the proper to the improper, the clean to the monstrous, the mother to the murderer. That which both fascinates and must be expelled.

And so the question must be asked again of the very real–everyday, political, lived—Chamberlain case: is transformation—of social violence, of the rituals of bloodletting, scapegoating, and abjecting at a social level—ever possible? Can the memory of the Chamberlain case effect a difference in the way Australians conduct their processes of mercy and justice? In the face of Kristeva's psychoanalytic universalising, it perhaps seems a naïve question. Are societies—pre-modern and so-called modern—inevitably driven to such rituals of perpetual scapegoating?

Perpetual scapegoating?

According to Girard, and before him Mary Douglas, so-called modern societies with their sophisticated legal procedures are in no way exempt from the sacred demand for release from guilt. Girardian critic Stephen Kaufmann takes up this question:

> What about 'civilized' cultures? They are not free of sacred violence, but it tends to be more hidden, for at least two reasons. First, courts of law have generated order in 'civilized' societies such that there appears to be no need for scapegoating to maintain social order. If someone feels slighted, they may take the issue to a supposedly impartial court, and peaceful resolution is possible in ways that are often not available to primal cultures. The need for sacred violence therefore appears reduced. In truth, judges have become the high priests, rendering judgment and punishing wrongdoers. A Girardian analysis still points to sacred violence at the origin of differentiating 'good' from 'bad,' from which the law derives.[18]

18. Stephen R Kaufman, 'Christianity and the Problem of Human Violence', at <www.all-creatures.org/living/cphv-030.html>. Accessed May 30, 2005.

This paper has been arguing that it is important to recognise Lindy Chamberlain, and to a lesser extent her family, as scapegoats of Australian culture's sacred violence. Often Girard, especially in his earlier works, speaks and writes as if such mechanisms are inevitably and simply repetitious, and that all societies are prone to this 'storage of violent energy which tends towards explosion and . . . In order for this violence to be deferred there must be a collective transference against a collective victim that can be completely arbitrary and against whom all tensions are projected, the scapegoat'.[19] If we accept Girard's basic premises (as historical, and/or metaphorical), we are able to consider 'modern' societies, just as much as overtly religious cultures, now and in the past, as gripped and impelled by such mechanisms. It would take another essay, at least, to open up Girard's and others' arguments regarding the possibility of transformation of such mechanisms in the modern era.

At a more popular level of discourse, but similarly attempting to think about what purpose Lindy Chamberlain's scapegoating served for Australian society, the anonymous Australian author of the *onemansweb* blog site wrote on the topic:

> Lindy Chamberlain offered us a wonderful opportunity. We could vent all our rage about children, and all our guilt, on this woman who was telling such an 'unlikely' story. She was the ideal candidate for a scapegoat: female, not showing enough grief, a member of a strange religious group. We could safely tip all our hatred, prejudice and anger on her—as journalist, police, or the ever expert general public.

While oneman has a gender-inflected argument here, it is important to note that his fuller discussion also embraces the Australian treatment of 'disgraced' Governor-General Hollingsworth and what oneman calls 'the howls for his resignation', and the 'baying on commercial radio talkback'. Scapegoating in the case of Lindy Chamberlain does of course have a very different orientation and set of circumstances. However, the same operations of social violence were observable in the case of former Bishop Hollingsworth, who before he was submitted to any civic legal inspection was caught up in highly emotional and explosive declarations of his guilt. As a religious figure accused of being at the very least 'passive' in regard to the Anglican church's abuse of children, he was constantly described as culpa-

19. Girard quoted in Müller, 'Interview'.

ble by the broader populace. In common with many societies, Australians have a history of vociferously calling for blood when the inflaming issue of the safety of children, in relation to the institutions of religion, is seen to be at stake, as they were in both the Chamberlain and the Hollingsworth cases.

Logos of violence, logos of love

It has been possible to show that the Lindy Chamberlain case affirms, or even exemplifies, the central and arguably pessimistic thesis of perpetual scapegoating. Such arguments suggest that the practice continues in contemporary Australian society. However, in the context of the subsequent actions of individuals of good will, in parts of the Australian legal system and more generally, of those who were able to interpret acts of scapegoating in the Chamberlain case and to deconstruct its mechanisms in multiple ways, can Australians, in John Bryson's words, acknowledge the cost and the wrong path taken. Can we hope that this critical reflexivity and self-knowledge might act as a counterbalance to the worst effects of scapegoating? In his later view of sacred violent repetition, Girard does offer some more hopeful arguments. His 1987 work, *Things Hidden since the Foundation of the World*[20] points to this capacity for societies' to understand their own violent sources. For Girard, such cultural self-knowledge comes slowly however, through revelation:

> The Logos of love puts up no resistance; it always allows itself to be expelled by the Logos of violence. But its expulsion is revealed in a more and more obvious fashion, and by the same process the Logos of violence is revealed as what can only exist by expelling the true Logos and feeding upon it in one way or another.[21]

Articulated in broad theological terms, Girard's argument might be too close to Christian dogma. At the everyday level of individuals and cultures, this understanding of the struggle between 'the Logos of love' and the 'Logos of violence' might make little sense, might seem *merely* metaphoric, or mystical. Certainly the living woman, Lindy Chamberlain, did not go peacefully or without a murmur—under the sign of love—into prison.

20. René Girard, *Things Hidden Since the Foundation of the World* (Stanford: Stanford University Press, 1987).
21. Girard, *Things Hidden*, 274.

She and her supporters waged vigorous resistance legally and through the media, against the violence to which she saw herself and her family being subjected. This resistance necessarily took place in a cultural context in which violent and subterranean as well as overt religious and sexual stereotyping was rife; and on terms already decreed by the 'modern' society of which she was a citizen: the institutions of its policing, law, mass media, scientific knowledge. Such institutions, still trailing their enlightenment beliefs, most often define themselves as operating impartially—believing themselves to be at some remove from the perceived extremes both of 'the Logos of love' and the 'Logos of violence'.

Twenty-eight years later we can now reflect on what we have learned from 'the Chamberlain case': from the life, expressed feelings, beliefs, actions and experiences of Lindy Chamberlain the woman, her daughter Azaria, her husband Michael, and their three other children, who were turned violently by their society into scapegoats. There will be individual responses to this drama, but at the level of the culture Girard's theory rings true here. Has the nature of the drama played out between 'The Logos of love' and 'The Logos of violence' become clearer in the intervening years? Can the Chamberlain case stand as a memorial, an accrual of wisdom, so that the very institutions of this culture might be changed and empowered to acknowledge the horror and farce of violence and scapegoating to which it is so ineluctably and repeatedly drawn?

The final, though belated, liberation and legal vindication of Lindy Chamberlain may make us feel something of that new possibility. However, in the larger context of Australia's actions towards its indigenous peoples, and towards the many refugees who have sought asylum in this modern nation, it seems that scapegoating—the militant protecting of the borders of the self and the community against perceived violences without and within—continues, driven so often by potent, archaic forces. The February 2008 Apology to the members of the indigenous stolen generation, delivered on behalf of the Australian Federal Government by Prime Minister Kevin Rudd, might be read in this larger context of sacred violence, as a new, more hopeful public ritual that seeks to address the repetitions of the past. Time will tell.

Works Cited

Bryson, John. 'The search for a culprit continues', *Sydney Morning Herald*, 16/12/1995: *News and Features*: 21.

Douglas, Mary, *Purity and Danger* (2002) New York: Routledge.

Durkheim, Emile. *The Elementary Forms of Religious Life* (1912), translated by Swain, Joseph (London: Allen and Unwin, 1963).

Eliade, Mircea. *The Sacred and the Profane: the nature of Religion*, translated by Trask, Willard R (New York : Harcourt Brace Jovanovich, 1957).

Enker, Debi. 'Trial by Fury', *Sydney Morning Herald*, 22/1/2004: *The Guide*: 4

Girard, René. *Violence and the Sacred* (London and New York: Continuum, 1970/2005).

----*The Scapegoat,* translated by Freccero, Yvonne (Baltimore: The Johns Hopkins University Press, 1982/1986).

----*Things Hidden since the Foundation of the World* (Stanford: Stanford University Press. 1987).

Kaufman, Stephen R. (2005) 'Christianity and the Problem of Human Violence', http://www.all-creatures.org/living/cphv-030.html Accessed May, 2005.

Kristeva, Julia. *In the Beginning Was Love: Psychoanalysis and Faith*, translated by Goldhammer, Arthur (New York: Columbia University Press, 1987).

----*Powers of Horror* (New York: Columbia University Press, 1982).

McKenna, Andrew J. *Violence and Difference: Girard, Derrida, and Deconstruction* (Chicago: University of Illinois Press, 1992).

Müller, Markus (1996) 'Interview with René Girard', *Anthropoetics* II, no. 1 (June 1996). http://www.anthropoetics.ucla.edu/AP0201/interv.htm (Accessed April 2005).

onemansweb.org/jan/ politics/ethics-scapegoat.htm (Accessed April 2005).

Otto, Rudolf. *The idea of the Holy: An Inquiry into the Non-rational Factor in the Idea of the Divine and its Relation to the Rational,* translated by Harvey, John W (New York: Oxford University Press, 1933/1950).

Peterson, Thomas V. (1989) Review of *Things Hidden Since the Foundation of the World* by René Girard, *Journal of the American Academy of Religion*, 57/3, (Autumn 1989): 643–645.

Reineke, Martha J. 'The Mother in Mimesis: Kristeva and Girard on Violence and the Sacred', in *Body/Text in Julia Kristeva: Religion, Women, and Psychoanalysis*, edited by Crownfield, David R (Albany, NY: State University of New York Press, 1992), 67–85.

Index

C